Manage Your Stress for a Happier Life

Terry Looker and
Olga Gregson

For UK order enquiries: please contact Bookpoint Ltd,
130 Milton Park, Abingdon, Oxon OX14 4SB.
Telephone: +44 (0) 1235 827720. Fax: +44 (0) 1235 400454.
Lines are open 09.00–17.00, Monday to Saturday, with a 24-hour
message answering service. Details about our titles and how to
order are available at www.teachyourself.com

For USA order enquiries: please contact McGraw-Hill Customer
Services, PO Box 545, Blacklick, OH 43004-0545, USA.
Telephone: 1-800-722-4726. Fax: 1-614-755-5645.

For Canada order enquiries: please contact McGraw-Hill
Ryerson Ltd, 300 Water St, Whitby, Ontario L1N 9B6, Canada.
Telephone: 905 430 5000. Fax: 905 430 5020.

Long renowned as the authoritative source for self-guided learning –
with more than 50 million copies sold worldwide – the
Teach Yourself series includes over 500 titles in the fields of
languages, crafts, hobbies, business, computing and education.

British Library Cataloguing in Publication Data: a catalogue record
for this title is available from the British Library.

Library of Congress Catalog Card Number: on file.

First published in UK 1997 by Hodder Education, part of
Hachette UK, 338 Euston Road, London NW1 3BH.

First published in US 1997 by The McGraw-Hill Companies, Inc.

This edition published 2010.

Previously published as *Teach Yourself Managing Stress*

The **Teach Yourself** name is a registered trade mark of
Hodder Headline.

Copyright © 1997, 2003, 2008, 2010 Terry Looker and
Olga Gregson

The publisher has used its best endeavours to ensure that the URLs
for external websites referred to in this book are correct and active
at the time of going to press. However, the publisher and the
author have no responsibility for the websites and can make no
guarantee that a site will remain live or that the content will remain
relevant, decent or appropriate.

Hachette UK's policy is to use papers that are natural, renewable
and recyclable products and made from wood grown in sustainable
forests. The logging and manufacturing processes are expected to
conform to the environmental regulations of the country of origin.

Impression number	10 9 8 7 6 5 4
Year	2014 2013

Acknowledgements

We are very grateful to the late Dr Meyer Friedman and the staff of the Recurrent Coronary Prevention Project, Meyer Friedman Institute, San Francisco for providing us with the opportunity to work in the area of stress management.

We also thank our many friends and acquaintances in the United States for their encouragement and time to discuss their work. We would like to express our thanks particularly to Dr Larry Scherwitz and Dr Ray Rosenman.

Special thanks are due to our families for their love and support.

Image credits

Front cover: © George Doyle/Stockbyte/Getty Images

Back cover: © Jakub Semeniuk/iStockphoto.com, © Royalty-Free/Corbis, © agencyby/iStockphoto.com, © Andy Cook/iStockphoto.com, © Christopher Ewing/iStockphoto.com, © zebicho – Fotolia.com, © Geoffrey Holman/iStockphoto.com, © Photodisc/Getty Images, © James C. Pruitt/iStockphoto.com, © Mohamed Saber – Fotolia.com

Contents

Important notice to readers

Before following any advice given in this book, readers are
urged to consider their current health status and to consult their
doctor if in any doubt. This is particularly important for those
with circulatory problems. The authors do not accept legal
responsibility for any consequences arising from the information
and advice described herein.

Meet the authors

This book is based on our stress awareness and management programme *Stresswise*. We developed this programme from our combined knowledge and experience in human physiology and behaviour, and also from our many years as University teachers.

We have presented our *Stresswise* programme to numerous and varied organizations throughout the UK. This book started as a set of single page handouts that we gave to our course participants throughout the programme. At one course a man suggested we put the handouts together, add some more detail, and produce a course manual for participants to take away. We produced the manual which grew in size over the years until we eventually decided that there was now enough material to convert it into a self-help book. So the first edition of this book was titled *Stresswise*, and then a later edition, *Managing Stress*, and then it was adapted for the *Teach Yourself* series.

Our aim was to write an easy to understand guide based on the biology of the stress response, and then to show how this response can be influenced by techniques and lifestyle activities, in order that individuals can manage their stress effectively. We were thrilled when Professor Louis Appleby CBE then as National Director of Mental Health, and now National Clinical Director for Health and Criminal Justice, reviewed our book on BBC Radio 4, saying about the previous edition:

> **Managing Stress** *is one of the better self-help buys; it offers down to earth advice on relaxing and adjusting to demands of daily life... it is scientifically sound and more or less purged of scientific jargon.*

We had achieved our aim. Since then we have received many letters from readers and stress management and health practitioners saying how helpful in understanding and dealing with stress our book has been for them. We hope you find it helpful too.

Foreword

It is common knowledge that uncontrolled stress can trigger many diseases and disorders: from insomnia, gastric ulcers, high blood pressure, asthma and migraine to depression and chronic fatigue. For a long time, however, such problems were treated as something over which we could exercise no control. It was assumed that you could only treat their symptoms with drugs; treat the stress that triggered them with more drugs, and hope for the best.

Now, thanks to research into altered states of consciousness, deep relaxation, self-awareness and biofeedback, we know that we can exercise control over our responses and, once we have gained enough self-awareness and tucked a few stress management skills under our belts, virtually choose how we wish to meet the challenges of our day-to-day lives.

Stress is not some great dark threat over which we as helpless human beings can exercise little influence. Yet too often in books and articles it is still portrayed that way. In fact, so much nonsense has been written about stress in the industrialized world that it is a pleasure to see the *Stresswise* programme appear in print. Not only does the book avoid the pitfalls of so many of its predecessors it also presents a clear, concise and practical account of what stress really is and how to make a friend of it instead of letting it destroy you.

Looker and Gregson are professionals who have done their homework well and know their stuff. But they have other traits in common which endears the book to its reader as well: compassion, for instance. They genuinely care about life and about helping each and every human being live it to the full. They also have a sense of humour. They completely avoid the pomposity which too often creeps into books of this kind. Interesting, thorough and useful, this is a book I can heartily recommend to anyone determined to find out about how to make stress work for you rather than against you.

Leslie Kenton, Natural Health and Beauty Expert

Only got a minute?

Then this book is definitely for you!

Learning how to handle demands, challenges and threats more effectively results in improved coping ability, stress management skills and better quality of life.

This means we become:

▸ less time urgent

▸ less hostile

▸ less angry

▸ less aggressive...

...all qualities that, too much of, are known to adversely affect our performance, relationships and health.

To improve our chances for a successful life-work balance, we need to know:

▸ how our mind and body respond to stress

▸ how to identify potential for stress

▸ about training skills to increase our personal reserves and resources for dealing with stress.

No learning process can be successful without feedback – a review of the application of our progress, with continuous adjustment and refinement to what has been learned. This form of self reflection focuses on the learning process itself. It is not the same as the mistaken view of introspection as an excuse for self-pity. The aim of self reflection is for a reasoned, balanced view of life.

5 Only got five minutes?

Stress management is all about getting to grips with better awareness of what stress is. We must appreciate the fact that:

- we create our own stress, therefore, it follows that we can also alter our own stress
- what is stress for one person, may not be stress for another
- what causes stress one day may not cause stress the next
- what seems stressful initially may change over time
- stress results from our everyday life and is normal
- to a large extent, our lifestyle contributes to stress
- our genes and personalities have a large input in shaping our final stress experience
- stress management is a natural part of being human
- we are all expert at managing stress
- we may need help to get through tough patches
- when we feel stressed we should not feel as though we have failed; it just means that we may not know about available skills or resources.

One person cannot possibly know everything in the human experience. That is why, as humans are social beings, it means that the sharing information about what help is available can increase personal well being through mutual, cooperative effort. Self help books, therefore, can provide a wealth of beneficial resource.

Terminology that describes stress is used in essentially two different ways, depending on the discipline involved. This has led to some confusion in understanding the stress concept. Psychologists see stress as the 'stimulus' (the demand, object, event or situation). They say: 'Stress leads to strain.' Physiologists, however, see stress as the 'response' – the end consequence by the mind and the body to a stimulus. They say: 'Strain leads to stress.'

This use of terms gives the impression of a circular argument, or a non-definition of stress. This need not be the case. As long as one set of terms is applied consistently, a working definition of stress can be developed successfully.

This book adopts a physiological approach using the terminology developed by Hans Selye (1907–1982) who is regarded as the 'father' of stress research. Selye used the term 'stressor' to describe the stimulus. Hence, according to Selye, '[the] stressor leads to the stress response'. Stress is seen as a response to the stimulus.

The stress response is continuously active; it is part of life itself. The kind of stress response activity varies depending on the stressor that activates the stress response. This is why the stress experienced can change, why it can become overwhelming and why the experience can be harnessed through learning and training.

The nature of the stress experience is determined by our experience and attitude regarding the stressor. For example, if the stressor is pleasant, the stress response is activated in a particular way that is unique to the individual experiencing that stressor. The stress experienced remains the same, or similar, for the duration of the stressor. The stress experience is manifested as an emotional, physiological and behavioural effect.

If, on the other hand, the stressor is unpleasant, the stress response will be activated in a response that will lead to a different outcome emotionally, physiologically and behaviourally.

In a situation where the stressor is life threatening or potentially life threatening, then the fight or flight response is initiated, followed by a defensive stress response whose job is to eke out energy reserves to ensure that there is enough resource to last out the duration of the life threatening stressor.

Learning about the stress response is the key to learning how to improve coping skills in stress management.

Introduction

What is *Stresswise*?

This book is based on our stress awareness and management programme, *Stresswise*, which tackles stress from its biological roots. The programme teaches the individual how to develop skills to reduce the bad and undesirable aspects of stress, avoid the ugly, and harness the good and beneficial side of stress. In other words, as the name *Stresswise* suggests, this book is a practical guide on how to become wise or knowledgeable about stress and wise or sensible about how to deal with stress.

Our aim is to provide an easy-to-follow, Teach Yourself programme designed to help you deal effectively with stress. This programme was developed from our experience as lecturers and researchers in human stress, performance and health; from studying stress research and management programmes in the United States and from presenting stress awareness and management programmes to a variety of industrial, commercial and professional organizations and individuals from all walks of life.

Another book on stress!

When we approached our publisher with the idea for this book the initial response was 'Another book on stress – how is yours different?' The first part of this response shows that stress is now an accepted word in our vocabulary even though its precise definition is unclear. It also reflects the growing public concern over the effects of stress on the health of individuals, industry, commerce, professions and society. In fact, stress has been referred to as 'the twenty-first century plague', a description confirmed by the media coverage given to this subject. Hardly a day passes without the appearance of articles in the national press referring to stress. Scanning the newsagents' racks of popular magazines each week will almost certainly reveal features on stress. It is a similar story in professional magazines and journals, particularly business and management titles.

The scale of this attention and coverage originates from the increasing amount of academic research, studies and surveys on stress, health, work and performance. In fact, this research is now so widespread that several new scientific journals have appeared during the last decade to publicize findings. Academic and popular books dealing with stress and stress-related subjects have appeared in increasing numbers during the last 20 years, so why another book on stress and, as our publisher asked, how is *this* book different from other currently available books?

We decided to write this book for two reasons. First, the fact that stress is mostly an experience that we create for ourselves means that only we as individuals can control and manage our own stress. Stress management is a skill that can be learned. Although there are many excellent stress and stress management texts currently available, we feel that none provides an educational self-help programme suitable for any individual wishing to learn about stress and how to deal with it.

There are many books aimed at helping specific groups of people such as nurses, executives and managers, but what about everyone else? Stress affects everyone. There are many books that deal with specific areas of stress, such as work stress, but ignore other aspects. This may be useful to some degree, but stress permeates all aspects of our lives and should therefore be tackled in a holistic manner. So *Manage Your Stress for a Happier Life* concentrates on 'self' and our interaction with the environment.

There are also many stress management books containing numerous quotes and references to detailed research, which make it difficult to understand the stress concept and to develop effective coping skills.

So in writing this book we have deliberately avoided using too many quotes and detailed references to scientific studies.

The second reason for putting pen to paper was to satisfy the frequent requests from the participants of our many *Stresswise* stress management workshops for a workshop manual to act as a refresher and as a source of reference.

Do you need *Manage Your Stress for a Happier Life*?

Some people seem to cope better with stress than others. This is because we are different. Our upbringing and personality largely determine our attitudes and expectations. This, in turn, determines the way we individually deal with the challenges and demands of life. However, we can all benefit from learning more about stress and how to handle it. Admitting to yourself or others that you are suffering from stress is not a sign of weakness. Neither is it a weakness to seek help. Taking lessons to pass the advanced motorist test is not an admission that you are a bad driver but simply that you want to be a better, more effective driver. So, in the same way, learning how to manage, handle and cope with stress means you simply want to improve yourself and to be more effective in the things you do.

Stress is part and parcel of change. Change in our lives means variety. Variety is the spice and sparkle of life. Change also inevitably brings challenges, demands and possible threats. *We can all succeed in living a happier, healthier and more successful life, whatever our current state, if we learn how to handle these demands, challenges and threats more effectively*. To do this we must firstly learn how our bodies respond to stress. We must be able to identify the potential sources of stress and we should learn how stress can affect our health and performance.

You would not be alone in feeling that you are suffering from stress. Today, at least three-quarters of those who visit their doctor have a stress-related complaint and many doctors now consider that a significant number of illnesses and diseases are stress-related in some way. Unfortunately, doctors often do not have time to talk through stress-related disorders with their patients in order to get to the root of the matter. For example, many forms of anxiety and depression are treated with pills and medicines which, while necessary and helpful in the short term, cannot solve the underlying problem. Excessive drinking, smoking and drug abuse do not help either. Very often, people are unaware of the fact that with appropriate guidance they can go a long way in helping themselves to deal with stress.

The three sides of stress

THE GOOD
Excitement, stimulation, creativity, success, achievement, increased productivity.

THE BAD
Boredom, frustration, distress, pressure, poor performance, decreased productivity, failure, headaches, indigestion, colds, unhappy and disharmonious relationships.

THE UGLY

Ulcers, heart attacks, cancer, anxiety, depression, nervous breakdown, suicide.

Becoming Stresswise *is the way to maximize your own natural resources to reduce the bad and avoid the ugly sides of stress and at the same time take advantage of the good side of stress.*

The story of Frank

Frank joined a *Stresswise* course as a last attempt to deal with his emotional problems which had led him to the point of nearly selling his company.

He described his lifestyle and behaviour before joining the course: 'I am very involved in work, have no social activities, get frustrated with employees, have difficulty in delegating and letting someone else do my job, and cannot relax. I am lucky I have an understanding, loving and supportive wife.'

His wife Helen described him as 'totally disorganized, dashing about everywhere and getting nowhere. He is impatient, easily loses his temper over the least thing and does not have much tolerance with anyone. When driving, if a motorist did anything Frank thought he shouldn't have done then Frank made sure the motorist knew about it. He would even stop and hold the traffic up to tell them so. He drives from A to B in the shortest possible time.'

Six months later Frank described how his life had changed as a result of being *Stresswise*. 'I have calmed down considerably and control my temper much better. I drive more slowly and take time off work to do my own personal things which never happened before. At work I have delegated and left the responsibility to others and sit back and think before making a final decision. I threw my telephone bleep away and started going home earlier and did things around the house. I rearranged my personal commitments that were causing me considerable stress.'

Helen confirmed much of his evaluation: 'He still does not have a lot of tolerance but doesn't fly off the handle at the least thing like he used to. At work he has let people, particularly his foreman, do the job they were employed to do without interfering too much. He is much more content to spend time at home than he ever was. His driving is impeccable; he doesn't exceed the speed limits or lose his temper with other drivers.'

A year after starting the course, Frank has maintained his new lifestyle. He told the group, 'Since I started the course I have relaxed tremendously; I feel a different person. I was a workaholic when I first came on the course; I couldn't leave work alone. I've just been on holiday for three weeks, the first time in my life I've been away from work for three weeks. When my foreman lost a major contract I did not blow my top, instead I talked it over with him constructively. Since then he has pulled in a lot of work. I do not mind losing contracts if it means I feel the way I do now. You cannot put a price on how I feel now compared to a year ago. I have let go of the reins and let my foreman take the responsibility which I had never been able to do in the past. I make a real effort to get home earlier and do things I never did before such as gardening and preparing the evening meal for Helen when she gets home from work. My driving manner is much better. I drive slower. I see more of life; more of the countryside, I never thought I would get to that stage.'

Frank believes it was his newly gained awareness and understanding of stress that helped him find his own way to deal with it. He knew how stress was affecting him, how he could identify it in himself and how to identify the sorts of things that caused him distress. He was then able to employ the appropriate coping skills to deal effectively with his own situation.

Manage Your Stress for a Happier Life will assist you in doing this. We cannot prescribe a programme of stress management specifically tailored for you as an individual, but we can give you the knowledge and practical guidelines so you can decide for yourself what you need to do and how you should go about it.

How to use this book

Part one of this book contains a questionnaire from which you will be able to assess the stress in your life and how you behave when you are stressed. To get the most out of this book, complete the questionnaire before reading Part two. The questions are designed to direct you into thinking more about stress as it relates to you through Parts two and three of the book. Your evaluation of your responses to the questionnaire will help you identify signs, symptoms and sources of stress.

Part two deals with gaining an awareness and understanding of the stress concept. We provide a definition of stress, using a model which we call the 'stress balance'. We look at why stress has become a twenty-first century problem. Next, the biology of the stress response is explained so that you are aware of what changes take place in the body when you are stressed. The mental and physical signs of stress are identified and the ways in which stress can lead to ill health and poor performance are described. Finally we look at the sources of stress.

We have found that an understanding of the stress concept is a key factor in bringing about changes in attitude and lifestyle which reduce the undesirable effects of stress and promote its beneficial effects. An understanding of stress is crucial for the effective development of coping skills, which are dealt with in Part three of the book.

Part three describes how to deal effectively with stress. It is based on operating the 'stress balance' in order to achieve the right balance. This means altering demands and building up coping resources such as the ability to relax, learning how not to create unnecessary stress, to enhance self-esteem and the importance of love and support.

In Chapter 15 we provide a step-by-step guide to help you develop your personal stress management plan; it is based on the guidance and information given in Parts two and three. The plan will help you to assess the demands and pressures in your life, to evaluate the stress you are experiencing and to choose stress management techniques to follow in a constructive manner.

In following your plan, your intentions are to harness the power of the body's natural resources to enhance health, relationships and work performance.

This book is a self-help guide and has been written to help everyone. It provides a broad coverage of the subject. Therefore there will inevitably be aspects which are not dealt with in depth or are only mentioned briefly. So for further details and more information, particularly on specific areas such as occupational stress, a list of further reading is given in the Taking it further section at the end of the book.

We use many examples of situations or events throughout the text to illustrate the subject material. Since *Manage Your Stress for a Happier Life* is intended for a diverse readership there may be many instances where, because of differences in the reader's religion, race, social background, marital status, gender and so on, the examples and illustrations may appear to be prejudiced. There is no bias intended and we hope that readers will view any examples used in the widest possible context and apply them as appropriate to their own situation.

BE STRESSWISE *FOR HEALTH AND SUCCESS*

Wise means knowledgeable. Being *Stresswise* means being knowledgeable about stress so that you can learn the skills to:

- *reduce your risk of ill health*
- *enhance your family and social relationships*
- *improve your performance in the things you do*
- *increase your productivity and creativity.*

Managing stress is ultimately your own responsibility and in your own hands. We hope this book will help you. Good luck!

Part one
Stress check – self-assessment

Assess your stress

Take a pen and paper and answer the following questions to find your level of stress: choose one statement that best describes your response to each question and note its letter next to the question number.

1 *You are upset by your partner's or colleague's behaviour. Do you:*
   a *blow up*
   b *feel angry but suppress it*
   c *feel upset but do not get angry*
   d *cry*
   e *none of the above.*

2 *You must get through a mountain of work in one morning. Do you:*
   a *work extra hard and complete the lot*
   b *forget the work and make yourself a drink*
   c *do as much as you can*
   d *prioritize the load and complete only the most important tasks*
   e *ask someone to help you.*

3 *You overhear a conversation in which a friend or colleague makes some unkind remarks about you. Do you:*
   a *interrupt the conversation and give him or her a piece of your mind*
   b *walk straight by without giving it much thought*
   c *walk straight by and think about getting even*
   d *walk straight by but sulk about it.*

4 *You are stuck in heavy traffic. Do you:*
   a *sound your horn*
   b *try to drive down a side road to avoid the jam*
   c *switch on the radio, cassette, CD or MP3*
   d *sit back and try to relax*

e   *sit back and feel angry*
f   *get on with some work*
g   *the question does not apply because you do not have a car.*

5   *When you play a sport, do you play to win?*
   a   *Always*
   b   *Most of the time*
   c   *Sometimes*
   d   *Never – I just play for the game*

6   *When you play a game with children do you deliberately let them win?*
   a   *Never – they've got to learn*
   b   *Sometimes*
   c   *Most of the time*
   d   *Always – it is only a game*

7   *You are working on a project. The deadline is approaching fast but the work is not quite right. Do you:*
   a   *work on it all night and day to make sure it's perfect*
   b   *start to panic because you think you will not complete it in time*
   c   *present your best in the time available without losing sleep over it.*

8   *Someone else tidies up your room/office/garage/workshop and never puts the items/furniture back in the original place. Do you:*
   a   *mark the position of each item and ask the person to put it back exactly where it should be*
   b   *move everything back to its original position after the person has gone*
   c   *leave most things as they are – you do not mind the occasional shift-round.*

9   *A close friend asks for your opinion about a newly decorated room. Do you:*
   a   *think it's awful and say so*
   b   *think it's awful but say it looks wonderful*

c *think it's awful but comment about the good aspects*
d *think it's awful and suggest improvements.*

10 When you do something, do you:
    a *always work to produce a perfect result*
    b *do your best and do not worry if it is not perfect*
    c *think that everything you do is perfect.*

11 Your family complains that you spend too little time with
    them because of your work. Do you:
    a *worry but feel that you cannot do anything about it*
    b *work in the lounge so that you can be with them*
    c *take on more work*
    d *find that your family has never complained*
    e *reorganize your work so that you can be with them more.*

12 What is your idea of an ideal evening?
    a *A large party with lots to drink and eat*
    b *An evening with your partner doing something you both
      enjoy*
    c *Getting away from it all by yourself*
    d *A small group of friends at dinner*
    e *An evening with the family doing something you all enjoy*
    f *Working*

13 Which one or more of the following do you do?
    a *Bite your nails*
    b *Feel constantly tired*
    c *Feel breathless without exertion*
    d *Drum with your fingers*
    e *Sweat for no apparent reason*
    f *Fidget*
    g *Gesticulate*
    h *None of the above*

14 Which one or more of the following do you suffer from?
    a *Headaches*
    b *Muscle tenseness*
    c *Constipation*

    d *Diarrhoea*
    e *Loss of appetite*
    f *Increase in appetite*
    g *None of the above*

15 *Has one or more of the following happened to you during the last month?*
    a *Crying or the desire to cry*
    b *Difficulty in concentrating*
    c *Forgetting what you were going to say next*
    d *Little things irritating you*
    e *Difficulty in making a decision*
    f *Wanting to scream*
    g *Feeling that there is no one with whom you can really talk*
    h *Finding that you are rushing on to another task before you have finished the first one*
    i *I have not experienced any of the above*

16 *Have you experienced any of the following during the last year?*
    a *A serious illness to yourself or someone close to you*
    b *Problems with your family*
    c *Financial problems*
    d *None of the above*

17 *How many cigarettes do you smoke each day?*
    a *None*
    b *One to ten*
    c *11–20*
    d *21 or more*

18 *How much alcohol do you drink each day?*
    a *None*
    b *One or two drinks*
    c *Three to five drinks*
    d *Six or more drinks*

19 How many cups of freshly brewed (not decaffeinated) coffee do you drink each day?
    a *None*
    b *One or two cups*
    c *Three to five cups*
    d *Six or more cups*

20 How old are you?
    a *18 or under*
    b *19–25*
    c *26–39*
    d *40–65*
    e *66 or over*

21 *You have a very important appointment at 9.30 a.m. Do you:*
    a *have a sleepless night worrying about it*
    b *sleep well and wake up fairly relaxed but thinking about the appointment*
    c *sleep well and wake up looking forward to the appointment.*

22 *Someone close to you has died. Of course you are very upset. Do you:*
    a *grieve because no one can ever fill that awful gap*
    b *grieve because life is so unfair*
    c *accept what has happened and try to get on with your life.*

23 *You have got into deep water over a problem. Do you:*
    a *reassess the situation by yourself and try to work something else out*
    b *talk over the problem with your partner or close friend and work something out*
    c *deny that there is a problem in the hope that the worst may never happen*
    d *worry about it and do nothing to try to solve it.*

24 *When did you last smile?*
   a *Today*
   b *Yesterday*
   c *Last week*
   d *Cannot remember*

25 *When did you last compliment or praise someone – your children, your partner, colleagues, friends?*
   a *Today*
   b *Yesterday*
   c *Last week*
   d *Cannot remember*

SCORES

Note down your score for each question and total them.

1 a=o b=o c=3 d=o e=1	**14** a=o b=o c=o d=o e=o f=o g=1
2 a=1 b=o c=1 d=3 e=2	**15** a=o b=o c=o d=o e=o f=o g=o
3 a=o b=3 c=o d=1	h=o i=1
4 a=o b=o c=2 d=3 e=o f=2 g=1	**16** a=o b=o c=o d=2
5 a=o b=1 c=2 d=3	**17** a=3 b=1 c=o d=o
6 a=o b=1 c=2 d=3	**18** a=3 b=2 c=1 d=o
7 a=o b=o c=3	**19** a=3 b=2 c=1 d=o
8 a=o b=o c=3	**20** a=o b=o c=1 d=2 e=3
9 a=o b=o c=3 d=1	**21** a=o b=1 c=3
10 a=o b=3 c=o	**22** a=o b=o c=3
11 a=o b=o c=o d=o e=3	**23** a=2 b=3 c=o d=o
12 a=1 b=3 c=o d=1 e=2 f=o	**24** a=3 b=2 c=1 d=o
13 a=o b=o c=o d=o e=o f=o	**25** a=3 b=2 c=1 d=o
g=o h=1	

EVALUATION

51–68: Your stress level is low. You show very few signs of stress. You are not a workaholic. You show Type B Behaviour and cope very well with stress generally.

33–50: Your stress level is moderate. You show some stress. You are not a workaholic but there is some tendency for it. You show mild Type A Behaviour and generally cope quite well with stress.

16–32: Your stress level is high. You may show many signs of stress. It is likely that you are a workaholic. You display moderate Type A Behaviour and do not handle stress very well.

0–15: Your stress level is very high. You show a great deal of stress. You are a workaholic. You display extreme Type A Behaviour and your ability to deal with stress is very poor.

Your stress level scores are based on some of the main themes developed in this book. Bear in mind your score and these factors as you progress through the guide:

▶ *signs of stress*
▶ *Type A Behaviour*
▶ *attitude to work*
▶ *attitude to life*
▶ *lifestyle.*

Part two

Awareness
of the stress
concept

1

Stress: a twenty-first century problem

In this chapter you will learn:
- *about the concept of stress*
- *the rationale for the effects of stress*
- *the fact that stress is not a twenty-first century problem.*

Stress affects everyone. It is a necessary and essential part of our lives, an inevitable result of the interaction between us and our environment. We need stress to be able to adapt to the continual changes of our environment and to keep us on our toes in order to survive.

Just as a car can be serviced and tuned for peak performance and to avoid or reduce problems and breakdowns, so too can our bodies be prepared to run smoothly and perform well. Such self-servicing includes learning the skills to deal with stress effectively so as to avoid the ugly side of stress, reduce the bad and promote the good. An essential step in this process is to gain awareness and understanding of the stress concept. This is what this part of the book is about.

To tune a car you must know how it works and be able to recognize the symptoms of both a poorly tuned and properly running engine.

Once you have gained this knowledge you must then acquire the
tools to carry out the necessary adjustments. You can learn the
skills to review, adjust and tune your behaviour, attitude and
lifestyle in Part three of the book.

Facing a new type of threat?

One way of looking at stress is to regard it as an adaptive response
by the body to changes in the environment. The stress response
evolved to enable man to deal with life-threatening dangers, for
example being confronted by a predator such as a sabre-toothed
tiger. Activation of this stress response very quickly prepared the
body for physical activity: to stand and fight or turn tail and flee.
This was obviously a necessary action for the survival of our cave-
dwelling ancestors. For early man in his harsh and inhospitable
environment, threats and demands were predominantly physical.
Satisfying life support needs was a struggle: hunting for food, keeping
warm and finding shelter probably took most of his time and energy.

Today, in our advanced technological and computerized world,
we live in a 'convenience' society. How easy life is now. We have
no physically demanding hunting trip; instead we just jump into
the car and drive to the store, park, walk in, select tonight's dinner
from the supermarket shelves, pay and drive home.

We can even avoid travelling to the supermarket altogether by
sitting at a computer and selecting our meal for delivery to our
door, care of internet shopping. Cooking is simply turning a switch
on the cooker or microwave; no strenuous gathering and chopping
of wood and then making a fire. We sit down at the dining table in
the comfort of a centrally heated house; no need to look over our

shoulder for danger while we eat – the lurking sabre-toothed tiger or a raiding party from another tribe are not there. How different it is today, or is it?

Let us take the above illustration and re-examine it. The scene is probably more along the following lines: we get into the car and drive to the shops but on the way we have to pick up the children from school, collect the dog from the vet and do a whole list of other jobs, only to find that the car will not start or we get caught in a traffic jam or we get a flat tyre. Arriving at the shopping centre we search for a parking space then once in the shops we get pushed and jostled by the crowds. At the checkout we queue impatiently only to realize as we are about to pay that we have left our purse or wallet at home.

These examples illustrate the kinds of demanding situations that each of us face at some time. Not only can we feel physically threatened, we can also feel psychologically threatened, by threats to our self-esteem, our security, our role in society and our relationships with family, friends and fellow humans.

Insight

We live in a world where the rate of change and the types of change we face have dramatically increased and continue to do so.

The queue at the supermarket checkout and the traffic jam represent the fangs of the sabre-toothed tiger and when confronted by these we respond just as if that tiger were there – by activating our caveman stress response. Having activated our body for an immediate physical response, there is often no need or opportunity for any physical action! We cannot hurry the queue in the supermarket or the traffic jam. We cannot fight the queue; we cannot run away from it either. So we become impatient and irritated; we become angry; we fume!

Because of the structure of western society, most of our time is spent in complex and often confusing social interaction. This interaction has become very complicated because of the effects of urbanization and the types of society we have created since our cave-dwelling days. Competition appears more evident today than ever before: competing for jobs, striving for career promotion. Sadly, in today's society we tend to get caught up in the 'rat race'. We become pulled along in a tide of emotional and social demands and at the same time we have to find work and earn a living or face redundancy and unemployment. So inevitably our stress response is activated whether it is warranted or not. Often we can find ourselves in a state of high alertness but without appropriate outlets for physical expression. Our body may become prepared for a fight if we see the boss as the sabre-toothed tiger, lurking behind his desk, threatening our self-esteem, career prospects or job security, but we cannot leap into physical action. We may feel angry and aggressive but cannot hit out or engage in physical contact. Instead we fume inside, hit the bottle or vent our anger on others – often our loved ones.

This is where many researchers and doctors believe part of the trouble lies: *activation of our stress response without the physical activity that is meant to follow can be potentially harmful to health*.

Threats to our self-esteem and the security of our relationships and jobs are the result of an increasingly changing society. So rapid have been these changes that our bodies and our biology have simply not had time to keep pace. Again it is here that our problem lies.

Insight

We are dealing with today's social demands by using a stress response designed to allow our ancestors to deal with physical dangers.

Today, the threat of losing a job, the struggle and fight to reach the top of the career ladder, the struggle to find employment, job stress, marital and family disharmony, loneliness and financial problems are some situations that can gnaw away at us over a long period. This means that our body defences are in a constant state of activation, albeit of varying degrees, in resisting these threats and demands. This can also lead to ill health and in certain cases, death. It is ironic that our body defence system, which developed to protect us, can be today's number one killer!

So it is not stress in itself that is a twenty-first century problem. The increased intensity, number, frequency, pattern and variety of demands placed on the body activates the stress response in a way that may ultimately become detrimental to health – this is a twenty-first century problem! So what is stress?

2

What is stress?

In this chapter you will learn:
- *a definition of stress*
- *about different states of stress*
- *about the stress balance: the basis of this guide to stress management.*

Stress can be good, bad and ugly

When asked to define stress, most people usually refer to its bad side. They describe stress as an unpleasant experience, for example, being under too much or too little pressure, feeling frustrated or bored, being in situations which they feel unable to handle or control, thinking that they are a failure, experiencing marital disharmony, bereavement or financial difficulties. What they are in fact describing is *distress* – the bad aspect of stress. This, left unchecked, can lead to poor performance, decreased productivity and ill health. For the individual, distress can give rise among other things to headaches, indigestion, frequent colds, neck and backache and unhappy relationships. For companies and organizations, distress is seen in terms of absenteeism, lost production, poor work performance, accidents, reduced creativity and lack of innovation. Distress can also be ugly. This is the more extreme form of bad stress, leading to physical disability or even death as a result of heart attacks, cancer, anxiety, depression and nervous breakdown.

On the other hand, some people describe stress as a pleasant, exciting, stimulating and thrilling experience. They feel completely capable of handling the demands they face and deliberately put themselves into challenging situations which they know they can handle. The stress they are experiencing is called *eustress* – or *good* stress. Tackling interesting and stimulating tasks, being creative and productive, achieving goals and desires and participating in competitive sports can be the joys of stress. Here, stress is working for us to improve our performance.

Insight

Stress is an experience which is unique to each and every one of us. What is distressful for one individual can be positively eustressful for another person.

Deliberately putting ourselves into challenging situations can be distressful as well as eustressful. Someone about to take their first parachute jump may be overcome with fear and unable to jump (distress). An experienced parachutist will jump without worrying about the potentially life-threatening situation and enjoy the thrill of the jump – but with their stress response in a high state of arousal they will be alert and ready to deal with any problems that may arise (eustress).

In this example, the situation or demand – the jump – is the same for both parachutists but each experiences a different feeling and level of stress. This is because each assesses the nature of the demand and their own ability to cope with it.

A definition of stress

Stress can be defined as a state we experience when there is a mismatch between perceived demands and perceived ability to cope. It is the balance between how we view demands and how we think we can cope with those demands that determines whether we feel no stress, distressed or eustressed.

This can be illustrated and explained by using a simplified model which we have called 'the stress balance' (Figure 2.1). It is important that you study this model carefully as it forms the basis of this guide to stress management. We will refer to it throughout the book.

THE STRESS BALANCE

In the pan on one side of the balance is what we see as the demands (shown as D) around us. In the other pan is what we see as our ability to cope or deal with those demands (shown as C). When we feel able to handle our demands then C will balance D. This does not mean, however, that the scales are necessarily perfectly horizontal. Because we are dealing with a psychological phenomenon, we do not know how much of C is needed to be in total balance with D. We do not necessarily have to have equal weights in each pan in order to be in balance. Rather, the scales should be seen as fluctuating up and down to some degree through a zone of balance, which we will refer to as the 'normal zone' (Figure 2.2).

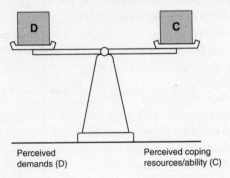

Figure 2.1 *The stress balance.*

The extent of this zone will be different for every individual and indicates that the body is operating in a normal and healthy way. In this zone we would not say we are experiencing stress. The normal zone can be regarded as our everyday living zone, or normal situations zone, in which we are dealing with familiar and routine daily changes in our environment and with everyday demands that, through our experience, we know pose no major threats. Our body adapts to the changing situation by activating our stress response to a degree that we are hardly aware of. In fact, if we were fully conscious of every little change in our body, we would be less effective in dealing with challenges, novel and emergency situations when these arise. So the stress response is always in a low state of activity, held in a state of readiness for further or full activation but without us constantly experiencing stress.

Of course there will be times when small changes in D and C will occur, perhaps as a result of inevitable daily hassles and not feeling too well, so the balance will tip one way and then the other. As long as these fluctuations are within the normal zone of balance, then we would not say we are distressed or eustressed but perhaps we would say we felt a little niggled or stimulated at times. It is when the balance tips outside the normal zone that we experience stress as distress or eustress, and clearly the greater the imbalance the stronger these feelings will be. Imbalance can occur in two ways:

1 *Alterations in perceived nature of demands*
2 *Changes in perceived ability to cope.*

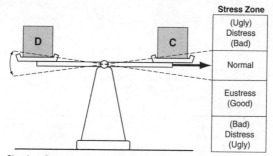

Situation: fluctuations in perceived demands and perceived coping resources but balance remains in the normal stress zone.

Figure 2.2 The normal zone.

Insight

Altering demands may not be easy to achieve, so altering the way we perceive the demand and building up coping skills so we are ready to deal with demands is the shrewd move for managing stress.

Distress

When we face an increased number of demands or view the demands that confront us as difficult or threatening, we need to make a judgement about our ability to cope. If that judgement is 'No, I can't cope', then the stress balance can tip into the distress zone as shown in Figure 2.3. Having too much to do in too little time; dealing with complex tasks without adequate training; promotion into a job for which we are not suited; having too many bills to pay and not enough income; worrying how we will manage if we lose our job; having domestic problems at the same time as changes at work – these are just a few examples of the kinds of demands that can lead to distress. Of course, the list could be endless and being *Stresswise* will help you identify those situations which put you in the distress zone.

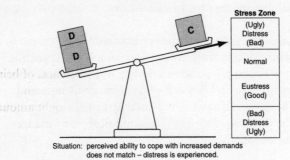

Situation: perceived ability to cope with increased demands does not match – distress is experienced.

Figure 2.3 The distress zone I.

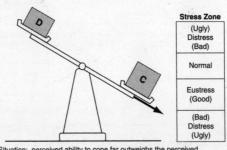

Situation: perceived ability to cope far outweighs the perceived demands; boredom, frustration – distress experienced.

Figure 2.4 The distress zone II.

Distress can also arise from having too few demands to stimulate you, resulting in boredom and frustration. In this case, perceived ability to cope outweighs demands as shown in Figure 2.4. Having too little to do or too few demanding tasks can be just as distressful as having too much to do or tackling complex jobs. This situation commonly arises when people retire or are given jobs which do not match their abilities.

Eustress

Eustress can be experienced when our perceived ability to cope outweighs our perceived demands as shown in Figure 2.5. Although we have an imbalance here, clearly this is a desirable one. In this respect, eustress can be regarded as an extension of the normal zone of the stress balance.

Notice here that the situation is different from that described in Figure 2.4 where distress results from having too few demands. The eustress situation gives rise to a feeling of confidence, of being in control and able to tackle and handle tasks, challenges and demands. The stress response is activated by just the right amount to provide the alertness, the mental and physical performance required to be productive and creative.

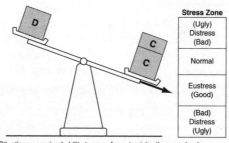

Situation: perceived ability to cope far outweighs the perceived demands; boredom, frustration – eustress experienced.

Figure 2.5 The eustress zone.

GETTING THE BALANCE

Because of the way we live today, we are almost certain to feel distress at some time or another, so we need to reduce the frequency and extent to which the stress balance tips into the distress zones. We can do this by decreasing the number and type of demands and by building up our coping resources. This will help to avoid or minimize the effects of distressful situations. We need to learn how to increase our excursions into the eustress zone by getting the right balance between demands and coping resources.

Insight
To get the right balance we need to reappraise how we perceive and interact with our environment because this determines the way we match up our demands with our ability to cope.

Note: When the term 'stress' is used throughout this book, it refers to any degree of activation of the stress response outside the normal zone, be it either distress or eustress. The activity of the stress response in the normal zone should be considered as an inevitable part of our lives and when in this zone we do not experience 'stress'.

We cannot live a life devoid of distress so the important thing is not to allow our stress balance to remain permanently in the distress zone and not to stray into this zone too far and too often. Instead we should aim to use our stress response to improve our lives and performance by keeping our balance in the normal and eustress zones. This can be achieved by learning the skills to alter the balance between demands and coping ability and this is the basis for the effective management of stress dealt with in Part three.

Insight
In order to learn these skills it is necessary to understand how the stress response operates in the body, what it does and how to recognize the signs and symptoms of distress and eustress.

10 THINGS TO REMEMBER FROM CHAPTERS 1 AND 2

1 *In order to manage stress effectively, we must understand what stress is, how it affects the body and how to recognize the signs and symptoms of stress.*

2 *Any change we experience is a demand that we need to deal with.*

3 *Everyone will benefit from learning how to manage their stress because we live in a world where the rate of change and the types of change we face have dramatically increased and continue to do so.*

4 *Stress response activation without physical activity, and in circumstances when it is not needed, can be potentially harmful to health.*

5 *Stress is a state we experience when there is a mismatch between perceived demands and perceived ability to cope.*

6 *Stress can be good (eustress) as well as bad (distress).*

7 *It is the balance between how we view demands and how we think we can cope with those demands that determines whether we feel no stress, distressed or eustressed.*

8 *Stress is an experience which is unique to each and every one of us. What is distressful for one individual can be positively eustressful for another person.*

9 *Alterations in our perceived nature of a demand and changes in our perceived ability to cope with the demand are the key ways to manage stress effectively.*

10 *Understanding our stress response makes it easier to learn the skills for managing stress.*

3

The stress response

In this chapter you will learn:
- *the biological details of the stress response and its various states*
- *the ways in which our thoughts and emotions influence various stress states*
- *the ways in which the stress response affects performance.*

Why you need to learn about the stress response

Almost everyone we have taught and counselled agrees that gaining an awareness and understanding of the stress response is an important and necessary step in the bid to deal effectively with stress. You need to learn about the biology of the stress response if you are to understand and appreciate how to recognize the signs and symptoms of stress, how stress can lead to health problems and affect performance, and the way in which stress can arise through the way we behave. More importantly, you will know something about the biological reasons for carrying out the coping exercises we describe in Part three, and you will also appreciate why these coping strategies have been adopted.

What follows is a very simplified general account of a complex response, much of which is not yet fully understood. We encourage you to read this chapter carefully. It will help you understand why you get stressed, how stress affects you, the consequences of stress to your health, relationships and performance and the reasons for practising stress management techniques.

What is the stress response?

The term 'stress response' describes a series of different and complex responses made by the body to any demand it faces.

Insight

The stress response is always active to some degree, operating within the normal zone of the stress balance to enable us to deal with everyday changes in the environment. When unusual, novel or excessive demands, challenges or threats arise, the stress response ensures that the body is always in a state of readiness to deal with them.

Because demands can be life-threatening, physical, emotional, pleasant or unpleasant, the body's response must be appropriate for dealing with the type of situation faced. It would not be effective and economical for the body to activate a single fixed stress response to deal with all eventualities, so different parts and levels of the stress response are activated to enable us to respond in the most appropriate way.

DEALING WITH LIFE-THREATENING SITUATIONS

If we are suddenly confronted by an actual life-threatening situation such as a car hurtling out of control towards us or someone about to attack us, our response must be immediate. The body goes on an emergency full alert and prepares for physical activity. Because of the speed and urgency of this level of response it has been called the 'alarm reaction' and also the 'emergency response'. It may be that running away from danger will preserve our life or it could be that staying to fight will be more effective. We decide in a fraction of a second which course of action to take.

The alarm reaction evolved to prepare our ancestors for action when confronted by a wild animal or similar threat. A split-second decision had to be made on whether to stand their ground and fight or turn tail and flee as fast as possible. So another name for the alarm reaction is the 'fight or flight response'.

DEALING WITH LONG-TERM DEMANDS

The alarm response is not an appropriate way to deal with long-term threats and demands. Here we need to make continual adjustments over a relatively long period of time. This involves mainly another part of the stress response called the 'resistance reaction'.

Many of the demands we face today are not necessarily directly life-threatening (life or death situations) but nevertheless pose threats and challenges to our personal security and wellbeing. These demands are usually emotional rather than physical in nature. Some arise unexpectedly and suddenly and last only a short time, while others persist for a long period – gnawing away day after day, week after week and even year after year. These long-term demands may include maintaining and protecting our own and our family's well-being and relationships, finding and keeping a job or earning a living and striving for promotion. Dealing with these situations is often distressful since it can involve struggling to establish control or fearing that control might be lost and, as a result, the safety and wellbeing of self and family is threatened.

How then is it decided which part of the stress response is activated so that the body can deal appropriately with the situation it faces?

Activation of the appropriate part of the stress response is the result of our assessment of the situation and how we think we can deal with it. This interpretation process then sets into motion a physiological reaction by the body to produce the right type of stress response. It is important to distinguish here between situations that are sudden, life-threatening ones, such as jumping clear of a car, and those which pose no actual physical threat to our life, such as being interviewed for promotion at work.

For sudden, life-threatening situations there is an immediate and total activation of all parts of the stress response. However, for situations which are more psychological or emotional in nature, the stress response is activated to an appropriate degree to enable us to deal effectively with the demands we face. In this book, we are dealing mainly with the latter category.

Another point to remember is that any expression of the stress response is based on either the alarm (fight or flight) response or the resistance response, or both. For example, the alarm response is usually triggered just enough to allow us to deal with immediate and short-acting demands which are not life-threatening, so we may experience a little aggression or a little fear. However, sometimes we may feel so emotionally threatened by a situation (whether or not it is warranted) that the alarm response is activated to such a level that we become quite aggressive – we decide to 'fight' mentally and our body is prepared for fighting. This is one way of coping with the situation.

On the other hand we may feel that the demand is too much for us to handle so we become scared – we mentally 'run away' from the situation while at the same time our body is geared for flight.

Insight
Emotions, for example fear or anger, play a major part in our interpretation and assessment of the situations we face and hence the degree and pattern of activation of our stress response.

Interpreting the situation
Basically we can interpret a situation in three ways:

▶ *'I can cope with this situation' – perceived coping ability outweighs perceived demands.*
▶ *'I am not sure whether I can cope with this situation' – doubt about perceived ability to cope with perceived demands.*
▶ *'I cannot cope with this situation' – perceived demands outweigh perceived coping ability.*

If we feel that we can handle the situation, the stress response is activated within the normal zone of the stress balance and we do not feel stressed. If we are uncertain about coping or if we feel unable to cope with a demand, the stress response will be activated beyond its normal zone giving rise to varying degrees of distress and accompanying mental 'fight or flight' or 'resistance' reactions. When we feel confident that we can deal with a demand, the stress response goes into the eustress zone. In this case, we often look forward to the challenge that a situation presents and as a result we experience eustress.

The differences in the extent of activation of the stress response within or beyond the normal zone of the stress balance depend on how you view or interpret situations around you and on how you feel about those situations. This means that stress is not in the environment but is a *state within you*. The way in which you transact with the environment determines how much and what type of stress you create for yourself.

> *Men are disturbed not by things but by the views which they take of them.*

Epictetus

Our interpretation of the nature of the demand and how well we feel able to cope with it depends on our experience of past events, our beliefs, attitudes, expectations and needs. These in turn depend on our genetic inheritance, personality, education, upbringing, age, sex and general state of health (Figure 3.1).

The body's response
Bearing in mind the interpretative processes going on, we can now relate how we view the situation to how the body responds physiologically to produce the appropriate level and types of stress response activation.

The appropriate response is ultimately achieved by altering the activity of the body organs to prepare the body for action. It is the job of particular chemical messengers in the body to alter

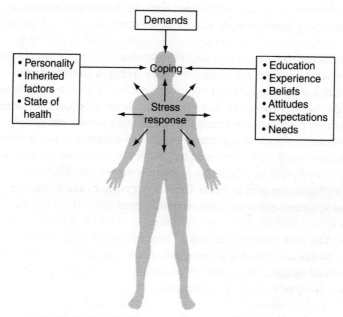

Figure 3.1 Factors affecting coping ability.

organ activity. Different messengers produce different effects; for instance, one particular messenger speeds up the heart beat, while another messenger may effect a decrease in the heart rate.

The type and number of messengers required for a particular task is decided by the brain after it has received information from the senses about the nature of the demand:

▶ *'Is it life threatening?'*
▶ *'Does it need to be dealt with immediately or can it wait?'*

The brain also assesses how we feel about the situation:

▶ *'Can I face up to it?'*
▶ *'Am I in control of the situation?'*
▶ *'I am angry about this.'*
▶ *'I am concerned about this.'*

The brain also recalls information from its memory store about what was learned in previous encounters.

- ▸ 'What did I do in this situation before?'
- ▸ 'This is a new experience; I'll have to tread carefully with this one.'

All these pieces of information are taken into consideration for a decision on the most appropriate course of action. Once a decision has been reached, it is transmitted to part of the brain, called the hypothalamus, which sets in motion the various chemical messengers required to bring about a response by the body. This response takes the following sequence:

- ▸ *On your marks* – 'Here is a demand I have to deal with.' *Brain collects information, processes it, assesses the situation and decides on a course of action.*
- ▸ *Get set* – Preparing to deal with the demand. Brain *(hypothalamus) activates stress response to a degree relative to the interpreted nature and importance of the demand.*
- ▸ *Go – Dealing with the demand. Type of resulting action depends on interpretation of situation and emotions.*

Let us take two situations and examine them in terms of what is happening within the categories of 'On your marks', 'Get set' and 'Go'.

EXAMPLE 1
Potential life or death situation. Confrontation by a bull about to charge.

On your marks
- ▸ *'Here is a demand I have to deal with.'*
- ▸ *'I see the bull. It looks threatening. I must get away quickly.'*

Get set
- ▸ *Preparing to deal with the demand.*
- ▸ *Body preparing to run.*

Go

▸ *Dealing with the demand.*
▸ *Run away as fast as possible. Full activation of the stress response. Heart beats harder and faster. Breathing more rapid and deeper. Energy stores mobilized. Blood directed to muscles. Muscles contract for action.*

EXAMPLE 2

Non life or death situation. This is a job interview which is not going too well. Emotionally, the interviewee sees the situation as fearful, and feels unable to cope. The stress response is activated to a degree that tips the stress balance beyond the normal zone, resulting in distress. The stress response is expressed in the 'flight' mode.

On your marks

▸ *'Here is a demand I have to deal with.'*
▸ *'I am not doing very well in this interview. I haven't answered the questions well and I've made a fool of myself. I wish I could get out of here as quickly as possible.'*

Get set

▸ *Preparing to deal with the demand.*
▸ *Body preparing to run but cannot actually run away.*

Go

▸ *Dealing with the demand.*
▸ *Mentally running away but physically having to stay and face the situation. Heart beats harder and faster. Breathing rapid and shallow. Muscles tensed ready for action. Blood directed to muscles away from gut. Stomach feels as though it is twisting and churning.*

Example 1 illustrates the activation of the stress response in terms of the flight aspect of the alarm reaction. The life or death situation, such as facing a charging bull, requires full activation of the stress response, directed towards the flight part of the alarm response to increase chances of survival. In this case the stress response is being used for the purpose for which it was evolved. Running away will hopefully save life. Each and every one of us has this response. It is there to help us survive.

However, the very same response is triggered when we feel like running away in a non life or death situation, such as that in Example 2 where the interview is not going our way. Here the stress response is not activated to its fullest extent because we are not dealing with a life or death situation. In this case the body is prepared physically to run away but this is not possible. We usually have to stay and face the situation. The desire to flee without the opportunity to do so produces a very different body reaction to actually running away.

It must be emphasized that all our responses to non life-threatening situations are varying degrees of activation of our alarm (fight or flight) or resistance responses, or both of these.

Insight

The problem in today's society is that in non life-threatening situations our emotional interpretation of the event is often inappropriate. We therefore need to learn how to handle non life-threatening situations so as not to tip the stress balance into the distress zone. Being *Stresswise* will achieve this.

In Example 2, for instance, the interviewee feels things are not going very well. He or she perceives that the demands of the interview now outweigh his or her ability to cope with the situation; the balance tips out of the normal zone and the person will feel distressed. The more the demands outweigh the ability to cope, the more the stress response is activated and in this particular case the more the flight aspect of the stress response is manifested in the interviewee's body actions. Here, the interviewee interpreted the situation as one to be escaped from and the body is prepared to do so.

These examples illustrate how the expression of our stress response can be related to our interpretation of the situation and to our emotional state. Although we know that our emotions do affect the expression of the stress response, the present state of knowledge of this link is limited. For example, depending on the individual and on the situation, a person's different emotional states such as anxiety, anger, fear, happiness, or no observable emotion at all, can result in similar levels of stress response activation.

We now need to explain what actually happens in the body during the 'on your marks, get set, go' sequence. You will then be able to identify the signs of your stress response and consequently discover the sources of your stress and how stress can affect your health and performance. You will also appreciate the basis behind the coping strategies and skills that are dealt with in Part three. So take a little extra time to study this next section.

On your marks

'Here is a demand I have to deal with'
Our senses pick up information about our environment and pass this to the brain for processing, interpretation and decision-making. We are on standby, ready to deal with danger, threats and demands. A demand arises; our brain assesses the situation and establishes how we can best deal with that demand. If we feel that we can cope, the stress response is activated to an appropriate degree and operates within the normal zone of balance. Activation of the stress response beyond its normal zone will occur only when it is judged that the demand cannot be handled (distress) or that it can be easily and confidently dealt with (eustress) as we have discussed above.

Having assessed the situation, our body must prepare for the appropriate action.

Get set, go

Preparing to deal with the demand

Once the brain has decided on a course of action, the 'get set' instructions are passed to the body organs, leading to an attempt by the body to deal with the situation. It may be that the decision, based on our interpretation of the situation and our emotions, is appropriate and our response is successful in dealing with the demands. In this case, we will feel no distress and may experience eustress.

However, it may be that the decision is inappropriate or our response to the situation is ineffective, in which case we will experience distress.

So how are the 'get set' instructions passed to the body to bring about a response to the situation faced?

There are two ways in which this happens. The first response is when instructions are sent from the brain along nerves to the body organs. This leads to a small amount of a chemical, called a **neurotransmitter**, to be released from the nerves onto the cells of the organs. This chemical alters the activity of the organ to prepare the body to deal with the situation, event or challenge. For example, the chemicals released from the nerves supplying the heart will alter the rate at which the heart beats.

The second way in which the stress response instructions reach the body organs is by special chemical messengers called **hormones**. These are released from special glands (endocrine glands) through instructions received from the brain. The hormone then travels in the bloodstream to the body organs where it alters the activity of the organ in such a way as to prepare us to deal with the circumstances we face.

Several neurotransmitters and hormones are released to initiate the stress response and each triggers a different set of actions by the organs.

Insight

It is the different patterns of body organ activity that result in either alarm response initiation, resistance response initiation or varying degrees of activation of both responses together.

The brain works out the most appropriate pattern of body activity to deal with the demand, and then sets into motion a sequence of events leading to the release of the appropriate cocktail of neurotransmitters and hormones to achieve this response. To understand how this happens you will need to learn a little about the brain and the links with the body organs via the nervous and hormone systems.

'GET SET' INSTRUCTIONS FROM THE BRAIN VIA THE NERVOUS SYSTEM

The nervous system is made up of about a billion nerve cells called **neurones**. Each neurone is connected to many hundreds of other neurones to form a complex communication system along which electrical nerve impulses are sent. Nerve impulses are the language of the nervous system and the means by which the brain communicates with the body organs.

The neurone endings do not have physical contact with the body organ. There is a minute gap between them so the message is carried by the neurotransmitter over the gap to the body organ. The neurotransmitter is stored in small packets inside the neurone endings. When an electrical impulse arrives at the neurone ending, the packets burst open releasing the chemical onto the surface of the body organ. When the cells of the body organ receive the neurotransmitter message the activity of the organ is altered.

The two parts of the nervous system

VOLUNTARY

We have a conscious, or voluntary, control over some parts of the body, including the muscles of the limbs and body wall. We can consciously instruct our arm or leg to move at will. The nerves from the brain to these organs form a part of our nervous system called the **voluntary nervous system**.

AUTOMATIC

On the other hand we have very limited conscious control over the activity of body organs (heart, stomach, lungs, glands and blood vessels). These areas of the body are controlled by the other part of our nervous system called the **autonomic nervous system**. This system works automatically to ensure that vital body processes such as the heart beating, breathing and digestion do not stop and are adjusted to deal with changing conditions. For instance, the rate of the beating heart is altered automatically to ensure that the right amount of blood is delivered to the muscles of the arms and legs depending on their level of activity – the harder they work, the more blood is required. The autonomic nervous system is involved in the everyday running and maintenance of the body's normal activities and is operating continuously – 24 hours a day, seven days a week, every moment of our lives.

Insight

The autonomic nervous system is of most interest to us in understanding how the stress response is activated, since changes in the level of autonomic nervous system activity produce the body actions necessary for dealing with demands.

When the stress response is operating within the normal zone, autonomic nervous system activity will maintain normal functions and enable us to deal with common everyday demands. Full activation of the stress response involves the highest level of autonomic nervous system activity. Where the event is not life-threatening, the stress response is activated enough to deal with the demand and this is brought about by an appropriate change in activity of the autonomic nervous system. It is the interpretation of the demand that will ultimately determine the extent of activity in the autonomic nervous system and hence activation of the stress response.

The sympathetic and parasympathetic nervous system

The autonomic nervous system is actually two separate systems: the **sympathetic** nervous system and the **parasympathetic** nervous system. It is mostly through increased sympathetic activity that the stress response is activated. The parasympathetic nervous system also has a role to play here because of the corresponding decrease in its activity.

The role of the parasympathetic nervous system is to conserve energy, to aid digestion and to defend the body from the invasion of foreign material such as bacteria. Increasing activity in the parasympathetic nervous system results, for example, in increased secretion of the eyes (tears), mouth (saliva), nose and lungs (mucus) and stomach (acid gastric juice). These secretions trap and destroy foreign material (Figure 3.2).

On the other hand the main role of the sympathetic nervous system is to expend energy. The body is prepared for action, for exercise and to deal with emergency situations by initiating the alarm response. Increasing sympathetic activity results, for example, in an increase in the heart rate, more blood flow to the muscles and quicker and deeper breathing (Figure 3.2).

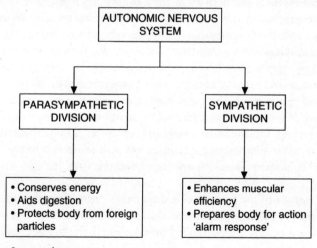

Figure 3.2 Summary of autonomic nervous system activity.

The action of the sympathetic nervous system is largely brought about by a neurotransmitter called **noradrenaline**. Parasympathetic action is mainly brought about by a neurotransmitter called **acetylcholine**.

Most body organs receive messages from both divisions of the autonomic nervous system. However, there are some which receive messages from only one of the branches. For example, the adrenal medulla, spleen and sweat glands receive messages from the sympathetic division only, while some of the salivary glands receive only a parasympathetic supply. This pattern of nerve supply distribution is important in determining body organ activity and allows a variety of different responses to be made by the body depending on the circumstances.

The table on page 42 shows the effect on body organ activity of stimulating the parasympathetic and sympathetic nerves.

You will notice that sympathetic stimulation causes increased activity in some organs, for example heart muscle, but reduced activity in others, such as gut muscles. Similarly, parasympathetic stimulation increases activity in some organs, such as gut muscles, but decreases activity in others, for example heart muscle. Where an organ has both sympathetic and parasympathetic nerve supplies, sympathetic stimulation increases the activity whereas parasympathetic stimulation decreases activity. For example, an increase in sympathetic activity while parasympathetic activity is low will result in a higher heart rate than normal. This is what happens if we increase our level of muscular activity, for example in exercising. On the other hand, an increase in parasympathetic activity while sympathetic activity is low will result in a lower heart rate; this happens when we are rested and relaxing.

Most organs of the body have a dominant control by either the sympathetic or parasympathetic systems. For example, the heart and blood vessels are controlled predominantly by the sympathetic nervous system.

Blood flow throughout the body is regulated almost entirely by increasing or decreasing sympathetic activity. The directing of blood to the muscles during exercise is an important aspect of the stress response as we shall see later.

'GET SET' INSTRUCTIONS FROM THE BRAIN VIA THE HORMONE SYSTEM

The other means by which the brain instructs the body organs to alter their activity is through the action of hormones released from endocrine glands. Hormones travel in the bloodstream around the body and therefore have access to all the body organs. Each hormone carries a specific message instructing the organs to alter their activity.

Of particular interest to us in considering the stress response are the **adrenal** and **pituitary** glands. The two adrenal glands, one lying on top of each kidney, are the source of several hormones which are released during the stress response. Each gland consists of two parts, an outer part called the **adrenal cortex** and an inner part called the adrenal medulla. The medulla produces large quantities of two very similar hormones called adrenaline and noradrenaline, technically known as catecholamines (pronounced *cat-e-coal-a-means*). The hormone noradrenaline is exactly the same as the neurotransmitter noradrenaline produced by the sympathetic nerve endings. In fact, the adrenal medulla can be regarded as an extension of the sympathetic nervous system. The sympathetic nervous system supplies nerves to the adrenal medulla and controls the release of adrenaline and noradrenaline from it. Although noradrenaline and adrenaline are similar in structure their effects on the body organs are different. This is important in instructing the body organs to prepare for either fighting or fleeing, as we shall see later. The other part of the adrenal gland, the adrenal cortex, produces different hormones that prepare the body to deal with long-term demands. One of these is cortisol which is of particular importance as far as the resistance response is concerned.

The effect of stimulating parasympathetic and sympathetic nerves

Organ/Tissue	Parasympathetic effect	Sympathetic effect
Heart	Decreased rate	Increased rate and force of beat
Blood vessels	Generally little or no effect but can cause dilation (widening) of blood vessels to heart muscle, lung, brain and sex organs	Constriction, except those supplying heart muscles, leg and arm muscles which dilate
Spleen	Little or none	Contraction and emptying of stored red blood cells into the circulation
Salivary glands	Increased flow of saliva	Decreased flow of saliva
Gut muscles	Increased movement	Decreased movement
Lung airways	Constrict, decreasing airflow	Dilation, increasing airflow
Sweat glands	Little or none	Increased sweating
Pupils of eye	Constriction of sphincter muscle; pupil becomes smaller (constricts)	Contraction of radial muscle of iris; pupil widens (dilates)
Liver and fat	Little or none	Mobilization of sugar and fat tissue
Brain, mental activity	Little or none	Mental activity increased
Blood	Little or none	Increases ability to clot

The release of most adrenal cortex hormones, including cortisol, is controlled by other hormones secreted by the pituitary gland, which lies close to the base of the brain. The pituitary gland is known as the 'master endocrine gland' of the body because it controls, by releasing its own hormones, the production and release of hormones from a number of other endocrine glands. The release of hormones from the pituitary is influenced by messages from the hypothalamus.

Cortisol's main role is to ensure a supply of fuel to active body muscles. It helps to convert stores of fat into energy. Cortisol also makes it easier for the catecholamines to carry out their roles. At normal levels, cortisol aids the body's defence mechanisms to deal with infection or injury.

Insight

The stress response is largely brought about by the action of the hormones noradrenaline, adrenaline and cortisol.

The brain sends out instructions to the body organs mainly via the sympathetic nervous system, ultimately leading to the release of noradrenaline from nerve endings directly onto the organ, and by hormones (noradrenaline, adrenaline, cortisol) from the adrenal glands via the bloodstream. In the case of noradrenaline this chemical messenger is both a neurotransmitter and a hormone. The reason for such an arrangement is to ensure that the body can react immediately when necessary by using the fast sympathetic nervous system communication line direct to the body organs. However, the effect of noradrenaline at the nerve endings lasts only a few seconds. The additional communication route to the adrenal medulla, releasing both adrenaline and noradrenaline, can prolong and intensify the response initiated by the sympathetic neurotransmitter. This ensures that the body response, once initiated, can be maintained for as long as necessary. In this way, physical activity can be sustained to enable the body to deal with and overcome the stressful situation.

When the stress response is no longer required, the brain sends instructions to reduce sympathetic nervous system activity and to increase parasympathetic nervous system activity.

The parasympathetic nervous system then produces acetylcholine which acts on the body organs and this leads to a state of rest and relaxation.

With this array of different neurotransmitters and hormones, it is possible for the brain to initiate the most appropriate organic action by selecting a suitable cocktail of chemical messengers.

How is the release of the various chemical messengers controlled?
The activity of the autonomic nervous system is controlled by the **hypothalamus** which receives messages from many other areas of the brain. One such area, called the **cerebral cortex**, evaluates the information from the senses and decides what response to make; for example, the decision may be: 'I can cope with this situation'. Another part of the brain called the **limbic system** adds emotion, such as fear or anger, to the response decided by the cortex. The type of emotion evoked depends on how the individual feels about the situation.

Insight
The limbic system colours or sets the intensity of the response decided by the cortex, for example: 'I feel angry about this situation' or 'I am scared of this situation'.

The final outcome of the interaction of impulses between the cortex and the limbic system is transmitted to the hypothalamus.

Insight
The hypothalamus translates the decision into a course of action by the body. It organizes nerve impulses to the body organs via the sympathetic and parasympathetic nervous systems, and hormone release into the blood via the pituitary gland.

'GET SET' INSTRUCTIONS AND COPING

As we have explained, activation of the stress response results mainly from the pattern of instruction organized by the hypothalamus and sent via two different systems:

> *sympathetic nervous system and adrenal medulla (inner part of adrenal gland)*

and

> *pituitary gland and adrenal cortex (outer part of adrenal gland).*

This is summarized in Figure 3.3.

We have seen that the expression of the stress response, or the way in which we deal with stress, has its roots in fight, flight or resistance. We describe below the physical effects of the three responses.

Get set to fight

When the decision is made by the brain to stay and fight, or when a sustained effort is needed to achieve control over a situation, the hypothalamus signals a mainly noradrenaline release via the sympathetic nervous system. It is the predominance of noradrenaline that prepares the body organs for fighting. Aggression, anger and hostility are the emotional hallmarks of fighting behaviour. This may first take the form of a sham attack aimed at frightening off the attacker. In animals such as the cat this may involve baring the teeth, hissing, showing claws, arching the back and adopting a threatening posture with fur erect. In humans we often see similar behaviours – making threatening noises and gestures, standing erect, showing and clenching the teeth. A sham attack can be an effective defence mechanism in itself since the attacker may call off his aggression or hesitate, think twice before attacking and give the defender the opportunity to strike first. If the attack is for real, the aim is to achieve control over and dominance of the situation. The body resources must be mobilized to provide maximal mental alertness and body strength. The stronger and more cunning of the pair of fighters will gain control and survive.

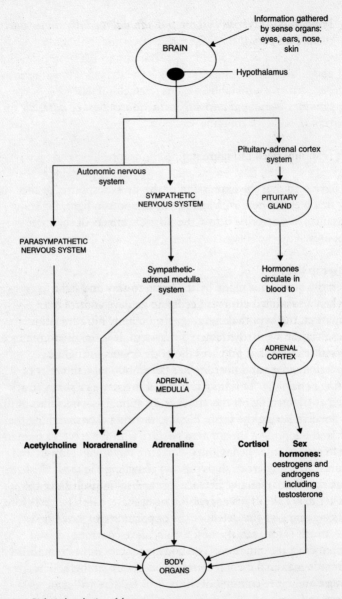

Figure 3.3 Biological mechanism of the stress response.

Get set to run away

On the other hand, if there is fear or uncertainty about how
things will turn out, or doubts about ability to take control,
a decision to run away may be made. The hypothalamus signals
a predominantly adrenaline secretion which prepares the body
for a fast getaway by increasing heart rate and making plenty of
energy available for muscular activity.

Both noradrenaline and adrenaline are needed for fighting and
fleeing. However, it is the emotion involved which determines
the predominance of either noradrenaline or adrenaline, and thus
the action appropriate for either running or fighting. This has
given rise to a great deal of confusion over the difference between
noradrenaline and adrenaline. Most people say, 'I can feel the
adrenaline flowing' when they are stimulated and excited. In fact,
it is noradrenaline, not adrenaline, which is associated with arousal
and gives rise to feelings of excitement and drive as well as physical
strength. For this reason noradrenaline has been named the 'kick'
or high performance hormone which in large amounts stimulates
special areas in the brain that produce a feeling of pleasure. In
contrast, the feelings and sensations associated with high levels
of adrenaline are not pleasant. Just think how you felt in the
dentist's waiting room or waiting for a surgical operation: that
was adrenaline at work, the predominant hormone released for
the flight response – you probably felt like running away.

Get set to resist

In situations where demands persist, activity of the pituitary–
adrenal cortex system is predominant. Here cortisol is important
in keeping up the supply of energy needed by the body for the
effort required in the face of long-term demands.

Maintaining the stability of relationships is a long-term demand
and this involves the sex hormone oestrogen and the androgens
(of which testosterone is the main hormone). Testosterone is
generally regarded as the male sex hormone, secreted by the testes.
It also plays a role in women through a closely-related hormone
called androstenedione which is released by the adrenal gland.

The sex hormones play an important role in our social behaviour: in forming relationships, bonding between the sexes and in mating. It has been shown that sex hormone levels in the body depend on how secure we feel and, for testosterone, how much dominance and control we feel we have in challenging situations. In situations where we feel helpless and a failure, levels of testosterone in the blood fall. This leads to poor motivation to do things and reduced sexual drive in men. High levels are released when we feel elated, secure and loved. This heightens sexual drive and motivates us into action.

GO

Dealing with the demand
When faced with a demand, the sympathetic nervous system initiates the immediate response mainly through the action of noradrenaline. At the same time, it stimulates the adrenal medulla to release its adrenaline and noradrenaline in order to supplement, sustain and prolong the response. These actions are geared mainly to provide energy for muscular activity (which increases alertness and strength) and to protect the body from blood loss in the event of injury (see Figure 3.4, page 51).

The first objective of the alarm response is to make available adequate oxygen and fuel for conversion into energy to power the muscle action. Extra oxygen needs to be taken from the air by the lungs and then carried by the blood to the exercising muscles. Sugar and fat stores must be mobilized to provide the fuel for energy production.

Getting the right amount of oxygen and fuel to the muscles
The heart beats faster and harder to circulate larger amounts of oxygen and fuel-rich blood to the muscles. The blood vessels supplying the active muscles become wider (dilate) to increase blood flow to its required destination.

In attempting to supply the muscles with the huge amount of oxygen and fuel-rich blood needed for emergency action, the body has a major problem to overcome. There is only a certain amount of blood in the circulation, so if more blood is needed by the muscles then there will be less available for other body organs. Some vital organs, notably the brain, heart muscle and lungs, must always receive a relatively large blood supply and usually this needs to be increased when supporting muscular work. Other organs are less vital in an emergency. The digestive system, kidneys and skin markedly reduce their activity during periods of stress. This means that their blood supply can be reduced, so the blood vessels supplying these areas decrease in diameter and become narrower (constrict). In other words, to supply the body muscles with adequate oxygen and fuels, there must be a redistribution of blood throughout the body – take from the non-vital areas and give to the vital.

OBTAINING MORE OXYGEN
Adrenaline dilates the airways of the lungs so that air will flow more easily in and out of the lungs. Breathing becomes more rapid and deeper so that adequate oxygen can be transferred to the blood. The oxygen-carrying capacity of the blood is increased by adding more red blood cells (the oxygen-carrying cells) to the bloodstream. This is done by the sympathetic nervous system: it stimulates the spleen which contracts, releasing red blood cells from its store.

OBTAINING MORE FUEL
Glucose and fats are quickly mobilized from the body's sugar and fat stores by the action of adrenaline and noradrenaline on the liver and fat tissues. Supplies are maintained by the action of other hormones, including cortisol, released during the stress response.

Increasing alertness and sharpening the senses
Noradrenaline enhances alertness and sensory activity: smell, hearing, taste, touch and sight. The pupils of the eye increase in size to allow more light to enter, thus improving vision, especially in poor light conditions. Hearing becomes more acute and the skin is more sensitive to touch, both clear advantages when fighting. Mental alertness increases, leading, among other things, to quick thinking.

Looking aggressive

An aggressive appearance is achieved by the erection of body hair and tensing of the facial muscles to expose the teeth. This, together with a general tensing of the body and the adoption of an aggressive posture, can give the impression of increased and imposing size aimed at frightening the opponent into retreat. Noradrenaline is involved in these responses.

Reducing activity of non-vital functions

While fighting and fleeing, non-vital functions such as digestion and urine formation slow down or stop.

Tensing the muscles

The catecholamines increase the tenseness of the body muscles, keeping them partially contracted ready to spring into action. Muscle contraction strength is increased, particularly by noradrenaline.

Minimizing blood loss due to injury

Another set of alarm responses is aimed at reducing loss of blood in case of injury during the attack or escape. Noradrenaline increases the speed at which the blood clots. This, together with the constriction of the blood vessels in the blood redistribution process, means that there is less chance of serious blood loss if wounded.

MENDING WOUNDS

Cortisol is released during and after the alarm reaction to reduce inflammation and assist wound healing so that injured tissues can be mended as soon as possible (see Figure 3.5, page 52).

Suppression of the allergic reaction

Cortisol suppresses the body's allergic reaction. This is beneficial when fighting or fleeing since dust and other irritants can cause breathlessness, runny nose and eyes and, as a consequence, reduced performance.

Both the alarm response and resistance response operate together to assist the body in defending itself. In persistent, distressful situations we might feel like running away but cannot. Instead we must stay and cope as best we can. This can lead to lengthy periods of cortisol release. On the other hand, when faced with a non-threatening demand that will not go away, we might feel like fighting. However, the nature of the situation may not allow it, so we bottle up our feelings of irritation and anger. This can lead to an overproduction of noradrenaline. Our feelings or emotions can and do affect the activation of the stress response. This is examined next.

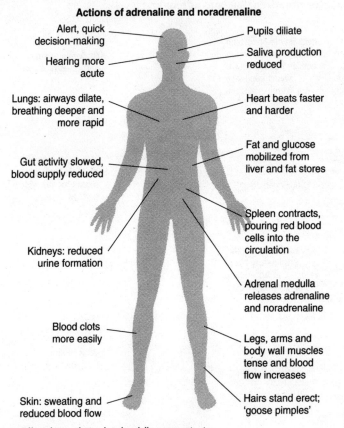

Actions of adrenaline and noradrenaline

Alert, quick decision-making

Hearing more acute

Lungs: airways dilate, breathing deeper and more rapid

Gut activity slowed, blood supply reduced

Kidneys: reduced urine formation

Blood clots more easily

Skin: sweating and reduced blood flow

Pupils diliate

Saliva production reduced

Heart beats faster and harder

Fat and glucose mobilized from liver and fat stores

Spleen contracts, pouring red blood cells into the circulation

Adrenal medulla releases adrenaline and noradrenaline

Legs, arms and body wall muscles tense and blood flow increases

Hairs stand erect; 'goose pimples'

Figure 3.4 Effect of sympathetic-adrenal medulla system activation.

Your emotions are revealed in your blood chemistry

To illustrate how our emotions are related to the levels of noradrenaline, adrenaline and cortisol, let us take two situations. A man flying from Heathrow to New York has a blood sample taken just before the flight. The sample was tested for noradrenaline and adrenaline levels. At New York he hired a car to drive downtown. Another blood sample was taken before he drove off and was again tested for noradrenaline and adrenaline levels.

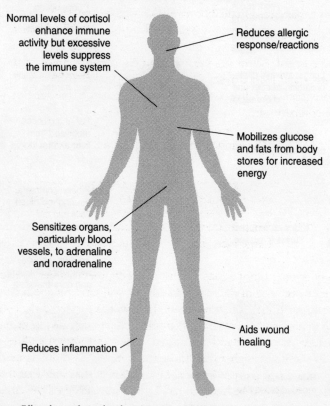

Normal levels of cortisol enhance immune activity but excessive levels suppress the immune system

Reduces allergic response/reactions

Mobilizes glucose and fats from body stores for increased energy

Sensitizes organs, particularly blood vessels, to adrenaline and noradrenaline

Reduces inflammation

Aids wound healing

Figure 3.5 Effect of sympathetic-adrenal cortex system activation.

From these samples, the levels of noradrenaline and adrenaline can be related to the way the man was feeling at the time. Where he was not in control of the situation – a passenger on the plane – his emotions produced the relative levels of adrenaline (high) and noradrenaline (low). Having reached his destination and probably feeling relieved to be on the ground, he got into his car, drove off and felt in control of the driving situation. Once again, his emotions were reflected in the levels of noradrenaline (high) and adrenaline (low). So the level of chemicals associated with the stress response is very much determined by our emotions.

Let us take another example. Blood samples were taken from two experienced male motor rally drivers before each attempted a rally circuit and again when they had finished. The blood samples were analysed for levels of noradrenaline, adrenaline and cortisol. Below are the results of the blood analysis of the winner and loser driver. The levels of hormones shown are those after the rally, compared with those before the start of the competition.

Can you pick the winner by looking at these blood analysis results?

Driver	Noradrenaline	Adrenaline	Cortisol
A	Small increase	Large increase	Large increase
B	Large increase	Small increase	No change

Rally driving is not a race against other competitors but against time. At the end of the race, each driver will have judged how well he has performed and whether he feels he has mastered the course. The winner's blood chemistry should indicate that he felt he had mastered the circuit and performed well, so his noradrenaline levels should be higher than those of the loser. Also the winner's adrenaline and cortisol levels should be lower than those of the loser, who would be likely to feel he had not mastered the circuit and therefore did not expect to win. So looking at the test results, driver B should be the winner. In fact he was. It is interesting to learn that the noradrenaline levels were higher at the end of the race for both drivers, reflecting the increased alertness and physical effort required for the race.

The chemical messenger league table opposite, and Figure 3.6 on page 56, summarize the relationship between how we feel and the release of the stress response hormones.

The power of the alarm response

The stress response allows us to produce extremes of human performance: speed, strength and stamina. There are numerous stories describing tremendous feats of power during activation of the alarm reaction. A woman achieved the strength to lift a car releasing her trapped child. A man racing for cover during an air raid did not realize that he scaled a ten-foot wall in his dash for safety. If there had not been an emergency, neither the man nor the woman would have had the physical strength to perform these feats.

Athletes and sportsmen use the fight response to 'psych' themselves up before races and events. Observe Olympic weightlifters. Notice how they pace up and down preparing to attack the weights as though it were a sabre-toothed tiger that they are about to take on in battle. Look at the aggression and hostility in their faces and behaviour. Ready for action, they grasp the bar, 'attack', and lift.

Athletes often drive themselves to the limits of human performance. To achieve this, they must reduce the pain that arises during intense muscle activity. When they continue to perform even though they should really stop, a group of chemicals called endorphins are released in the brain to suppress the pain associated with the body's efforts. Joggers and long-distance runners owe their sustained activity to endorphins which produce a euphoric feeling. This may be one reason why joggers say they feel so good after a run when in fact they often look terrible! Being able to pass through the pain barrier is essential for survival if we are in a life or death situation and need to continue our effort until we are safe.

Chemical messenger league table

Appraisal of situation	Dominant part of stress reponse	Chemical messenger(s) order of dominance
'I can cope' 'I am in control' 'I have mastered this'	Alarm 'Fight' aspect	1 **Noradrenaline** 2 Adrenaline
'This is too demanding' 'Can I cope?'	Alarm 'Flight' aspect leading to resistance	1 Adrenaline 2 Cortisol
'I fear failure' 'I feel helpless' 'I am not in control' 'I have failed'	Resistance	3 Noradrenaline 1 **Cortisol** 2 Adrenaline

EMOTIONS/ BEHAVIOURS	CHEMICAL MESSENGERS/ HORMONES	AMOUNT AND DIRECTION OF CHANGE FROM 'NORMAL' LEVELS
ANGER AGGRESSION FIGHT	NORADRENALINE ADRENALINE TESTOSTERONE CORTISOL	large increase small increase small increase little or no change
FEAR WITHDRAWAL FLIGHT	ADRENALINE CORTISOL NORADRENALINE TESTOSTERONE	large increase increase small increase little or no change
DEPRESSION LOSS OF CONTROL SUBMISSION	CORTISOL ADRENALINE NORADRENALINE TESTOSTERONE	large increase little or no change little or no change decrease
SERENITY RELAXATION MEDITATION	NORADRENALINE ADRENALINE CORTISOL TESTOSTERONE	decrease decrease little or no change little or no change
ELATION SECURITY LOVE AND SUPPORT	TESTOSTERONE NORADRENALINE ADRENALINE CORTISOL	increase decrease decrease decrease

Figure 3.6 Relationship between how you feel and some of the hormones released in your body.

10 THINGS TO REMEMBER FROM CHAPTER 3

1 *The stress response is the term used to describe a series of different and complex responses made by the body to any change or demand it faces.*

2 *The stress response is always active to some degree, operating within the normal zone of the stress balance to enable us to deal with everyday changes in the environment.*

3 *The stress response operates in two distinct ways:*
   ▷ *Alarm response: to provide speed and urgency in life threatening situations (also called the Emergency response and Fight and Flight response).*
   ▷ *Resistance response: to deal with continuous and long term demands.*

4 *When unusual, novel or excessive demands, challenges or threats arise, the stress response ensures that the body is always in a state of readiness to deal with them.*

5 *Our emotions, for example fear or anger, play a major part in our interpretation and assessment of the situation we face and hence the degree and pattern of activation of our stress response.*

6 *We are not disturbed by the demand itself but by the view which we take of the demand.*

7 *In today's society we face numerous non life-threatening situations which we react to as if they were threats to our life. We therefore need to learn how to handle non life-threatening situations so as not activate our stress response inappropriately.*

8 *It is the different patterns of body organ activity that result in either alarm response initiation, resistance response initiation or varying degrees of activation of both responses together.*

9 *The stress response is largely brought about by the action of the hormones noradrenaline, adrenaline and cortisol, neurotransmitters and hormones.*

10 *The senses send information to the cerebral cortex for evaluating what to do. The limbic system colours or sets the intensity of the response decided by the cortex. The hypothalamus receives information from the cortex which allows it to organize nerve impulses to the body organs via the sympathetic and parasympathetic nervous systems, and hormones release into the blood via the pituitary gland.*

4

....

Signs of stress

In this chapter you will learn:
- *about recognizing the signs and symptoms of the stress response*
- *about distinguishing between the signs of distress and eustress*
- *about looking for signs and symptoms of stress effects in yourself and in others.*

Recognizing the signs of activity in your stress response and identifying the position of your stress balance are essential if you are to reduce distress, avoid ugly stress and make stress work for you. Your knowledge of the biology of the stress response can now be put to the test.

_____

Linking the physiology of the stress response to the signs of stress

Most signs of stress can be explained by looking at the physiological actions of the stress response in the body. For example, a sign of stress is cold hands and feet. Why? The skin temperature of the hands and feet is determined by the amount of blood flowing into these areas, and when the flow is significantly reduced, the hands and feet will feel cold. There are a number of factors that can change skin blood flow, such as environmental temperature, but the stress response certainly does so. If you remember, there is a redistribution of blood flow in the body during the alarm response, taking blood away from non-essential areas and diverting it to the muscles and other essential regions. The skin is a non-essential area so the sympathetic nervous system sends messages to the blood vessels of the skin instructing them to constrict. This leads to reduced blood flow and therefore reduced heat, which results in cold hands and feet. Using this as an example, it is possible to explain how and why the signs of stress arise. By referring to the actions of adrenaline, noradrenaline and cortisol, described in the previous chapter, we show the effects on the body of stress response activation. It then becomes possible to explain what happens to the body when the stress response is over-activated and the stress balance tips out of the normal zone, giving rise to distress or eustress.

A LETTER OF DISTRESS

The following are extracts from a letter we received from a man after he read a news article featuring our work.

> *For almost 30 years I was employed as a Sales Manager for a local manufacturing company and during the last three years of my employment was promoted to Sales Director at a critical time in the company's history. At this time we were faced with 'cheap' (not necessarily inferior quality) imported products and in consequence the company could not compete and faced what became a slow but inevitable decline from 400 workers to 36.*

> *I was taking sole responsibility for sales. You can probably appreciate the attendant anxiety and frustration I personally experienced. Many were the long nights when I couldn't sleep, lying there worrying about how I could maintain sales, to arrest the decline of the company. Frequently sweating with anxiety and constantly aware of a heavy throbbing heartbeat in my ear when my head rested on the pillow. Severe angina forced me to retire early.*

Nowadays I find I am easily under stress even when doing simple tasks. <u>I have had to break off when writing this letter as I can feel tensions building up in me</u>.

I have not worked for four-and-a-half years and <u>see no prospects of becoming employable again</u>. Please keep pointing out to the general public the dangers of stress situations as I feel sure that some individuals will heed your valuable advice and hopefully will then not have to <u>suffer 'the indignity'</u> of being unemployed for the rest of their lives, as I have done.

The underlined sections describe some of the signs of bad and ugly stress, both physical and mental.

Assessing your signs and symptoms

Before we describe the physical, mental and behavioural signs and symptoms of distress, you can assess some of your own signs and symptoms by completing the questionnaire below. For this questionnaire, we have selected some of the more usually manifested signs and symptoms.

SIGNS AND SYMPTOMS

Tick the most appropriate box

During the last month have you:	(a) Almost never	(b) Some-times	(c) Most of the time	(d) Almost all the time
1 been easily irritated by people or trivial events?	❑	❑	❑	❑
2 felt impatient?	❑	❑	❑	❑
3 felt unable to cope?	❑	❑	❑	❑
4 felt a failure?	❑	❑	❑	❑
5 found it difficult to make decisions?	❑	❑	❑	❑
6 lost interest in other people?	❑	❑	❑	❑

(Contd)

7	felt you had no one to confide in or to talk to about your problems?	❑	❑	❑	❑
8	found it difficult to concentrate?	❑	❑	❑	❑
9	failed to finish tasks/jobs before moving on to the next, leaving jobs incomplete?	❑	❑	❑	❑
10	felt neglected in any way?	❑	❑	❑	❑
11	tried to do too many things at once?	❑	❑	❑	❑
12	felt anxious or depressed?	❑	❑	❑	❑
13	been uncharacteristically aggressive?	❑	❑	❑	❑
14	felt bored?	❑	❑	❑	❑
15	changed your patterns of drinking, smoking or eating?	❑	❑	❑	❑
16	changed your level of sexual activity?	❑	❑	❑	❑
17	cried or had the desire to cry?	❑	❑	❑	❑
18	felt tired most of the time?	❑	❑	❑	❑
19	suffered from any of the following more frequently – back and neck pain, headaches, muscular aches and pains, muscular spasms and cramps, constipation, diarrhoea, loss of appetite, heartburn, indigestion and nausea?	❑	❑	❑	❑
20	Do two or more of the following apply to you – bite your nails, clench your fists, drum your fingers, grind your teeth, hunch your shoulders, tap your feet, have trouble falling or staying asleep?	❑	❑	❑	❑

Total   ▭

Now turn to page 225 for how to score and evaluate your assessment. Make a note of your total score in the box on page 113.

Insight

The ability to recognize and monitor the signs and symptoms of your stress response activity is a crucial skill in managing stress.

Select the three highest scoring items and write these in the box on page 113. This will help remind you what to look for as you monitor your body's physical activity and your behaviour.

The brief questionnaire you have just completed does not address all the signs and symptoms, so we give a more comprehensive list below. Study the list so you are aware of the range of the signs and symptoms of distress.

Signs of distress

PHYSICAL

- ▶ *Awareness of heart beating, palpitations*
- ▶ *Breathlessness, lump in the throat, rapid shallow breathing*
- ▶ *Dry mouth, 'butterflies' in stomach, indigestion, nausea*
- ▶ *Diarrhoea, constipation, flatulence*
- ▶ *General muscle tenseness particularly of the jaws, grinding of teeth*
- ▶ *Clenched fists, hunched shoulders, general muscle aches and pains, cramps*
- ▶ *Restlessness, hyperactive, nail biting, finger drumming, foot tapping, hands shaking*
- ▶ *Tiredness, fatigue, lethargy, exhaustion, sleep difficulties, feeling faint, headaches, frequent illnesses such as colds*
- ▶ *Sweatiness especially palms and upper lip, hot flushed feeling*
- ▶ *Cold hands and feet*
- ▶ *Frequent desire to urinate*
- ▶ *Overeating, loss of appetite, increased cigarette smoking*
- ▶ *Increased alcohol consumption, loss of interest in sex.*

MENTAL

- ▶ *Distress, worry, upset, tearfulness, feeling deflated, feelings of helplessness and hopelessness, hysteria, seeming withdrawn, feeling unable to cope, anxiety, depression*

- *Impatience, being easily irritated and aggravated, feeling angry, hostile, aggressive*
- *Frustration, boredom, inadequacy, guilt, rejection, neglect, insecurity, vulnerability*
- *Loss of interest in self-appearance, health, diet, sex; low self-esteem, loss of interest in others*
- *Polyphasic (doing too many things at once), rushed*
- *Failing to finish tasks before moving on to the next*
- *Difficulty in thinking clearly, concentrating and making decisions, forgetfulness, lack of creativity, irrationality; procrastination, difficulty in starting to do things*
- *Being prone to make mistakes and having accidents*
- *Having so much to do and not knowing where to start so ending up doing nothing or going from task to task and not completing anything*
- *Being hypercritical, inflexible, unreasonable, over-reactive, non-productive, poor efficiency.*

You should note that this list is not exhaustive and some of the mental signs could be regarded as physical signs and vice versa.

Signs of eustress

Clearly, an absence of the signs and symptoms of distress indicates that you are not suffering the bad effects of stress. The signs of eustress paint a picture of how you might feel when you are harnessing the positive aspects of the stress response. You might feel and appear:

- *euphoric, stimulated, thrilled, excited*
- *helpful, understanding, sociable, friendly, loving, happy*
- *calm, controlled, confident*
- *creative, effective, efficient*
- *clear and rational in thought, decisive*
- *industrious, lively, productive, jolly, often smiling.*

Looking at the lists and thinking about your own experience, it is striking how many different signs there are. This is because the stress response involves so many body organs and activities. As was pointed out earlier, the stress reaction is a general response by the body to any demand made upon it. However, some body systems are more involved than others, for example, the heart and circulation, the lungs and the muscles. So when we ask the participants at our workshops to construct a list of their signs of physical stress, such things as awareness of heart beating, racing heart, heart palpitations (irregular beating), heart pounding against chest, fast shallow and irregular breathing and tense muscles are virtually in every column under 'distress'. So too are other signs such as sweaty palms, 'butterflies' in the stomach and a desire to urinate. Less commonly, we see items that describe general muscle tenseness such as jaws clenched tightly together, grinding of teeth, clenched fists and hunched shoulders, cold hands and feet. We believe there are two reasons for this. Firstly, most people do not usually associate these signs with distress and secondly, many people are under distress so much of the time that these activities have become habitual and are therefore never associated with distress. This raises an important point.

Insight

We must all learn to listen to our body and to read and take notice of the messages it is sending.

Similarly for the mental signs of distress, there are many items that would appear on most lists such as feeling impatient, rushed, irritable, frustrated, bored, neglected, helpless, tearful, worried, loss of appetite, overeating, loss of interest in sex, inability to concentrate and trying to do too many things at once. Others such as reduced ability to be creative, difficulty in making decisions and proneness to mistakes and accidents are less frequently listed. Interestingly, the mental signs list is nearly always longer than that for the physical signs. We are more aware of how we feel emotionally than of the physical signs that accompany these emotions. This emphasizes the need for us to take more notice of our body and to realize that what happens in the mind can affect the body.

Another interesting observation we have made is that when we ask participants to construct a list of the mental and physical signs of stress, their lists are made up almost entirely of signs of distress with virtually none for eustress. This illustrates the fact that most people simply think of stress as bad and do not usually associate creativity, efficiency, effectiveness, mental alertness and so on with the stress response. They never think of stress as being good when it saves our life and defends us from real harm. However, since such situations are few and far between, we tend not to recognize them nor use the benefits that the stress response can provide.

The outward signs of hormone activity

We have described how the stress response is mediated via different chemicals, notably noradrenaline, adrenaline and cortisol, so that different body actions can take place. It is possible to identify those signs in the body and mind which are produced by the action of noradrenaline, adrenaline or cortisol.

NORADRENALINE

Noradrenaline is associated with aggression and fighting behaviour as shown by changes in facial muscle tenseness and drawing back of lips to show the teeth which are clenched together. The back and shoulder muscles tense (hunched shoulders) and the fists clench. Hairs stand more erect; this is seen as 'goose pimples' since humans have relatively little body hair compared to other animals. All this action is to make us look more threatening and hostile. Also, the skin blood vessels constrict, and the palms of the hands, the feet and the upper lip become sweaty. The pupil of the eye dilates, mental alertness increases, thinking and decision-making become quicker and performance improves.

> **Insight**
> Noradrenaline produces a feeling of pleasantness and excitement in the absence of irritation, anger and hostility.

ADRENALINE

Adrenaline on the other hand is more orientated toward preparing the body for a quick getaway. Heart action increases and can be felt as a pounding in the chest. This is sometimes erratic and described as heart palpitations. Blood supply to the vital organs and skeletal muscles increases so it is necessary for noradrenaline to reduce the supply to the non-vital organs such as the gut and skin. This, together with a reduction in activity of the gut, gives the feeling of 'butterflies' and knots in the stomach. A 'cold sweat' is experienced when sweat is secreted onto the surface of a cold skin.

Insight
Feelings of uncertainty, worry, insecurity and anxiety are examples of the results of adrenaline activity.

CORTISOL

Outward physical signs that cortisol is at work are difficult to see although frequent colds, allergies or asthma could be indicators. However, the mental signs are clear enough: feelings of failure, helplessness, hopelessness, chronic anxiety, depression.

Recognizing stress in others as well as yourself

The main purpose of this book is to help you learn to recognize and manage stress in yourself. But it is also important that you can identify the signs of stress in others: your family, friends and work colleagues.

Insight
Being alert to the signs of distress in others will help you to reduce relationship problems and maintain a creative and productive office and organization.

At work it would be foolish to pile more tasks onto your colleague who is rushing around trying to do too many things at once and becoming impatient, easily irritated at trivial things and snappy with workmates. Or to ignore an overloaded colleague who has problems at home and perhaps withdraws, becomes uncharacteristically quiet and looks depressed. Watch out also for the colleague who becomes frustrated and bored because there is too little to do and who feels their abilities and talents are not being adequately used.

NOT ALL THE SIGNS ARE EXCLUSIVELY SIGNS OF STRESS

Care must be taken in interpreting the signs of stress since many can be due to other factors. For instance, cold hands can be due to winter weather! A low external temperature is a physical stressor because it activates the body's stress response, within the normal zone, so that a normal body temperature can be maintained. Unless the temperatures are extreme and potentially life-threatening, most people would not say they felt 'stressed' because of them. So a person might have cold hands but not feel emotionally stressed at the time. Furthermore, some diseases of the circulation can lead to poor blood flow in the hands, resulting in coldness.

Signs such as back and neck pain, headaches, muscular aches and pains, spasm and cramps, constipation, diarrhoea, indigestion and nausea can all arise for reasons other than stress. The symptoms of some diseases and conditions, for example Irritable Bowel Syndrome, are those we also see attributed to stress. It is when we find a number of these signs occurring together, in the absence of diagnosed health problems, that we can often attribute them to stress.

HIDDEN SIGNS

It is impossible for us to see blood glucose and fat levels changing, more red cells pouring into the bloodstream, blood clotting more easily or wound-healing processes being stimulated when the stress response is at work. These signs are hidden from our eyes but not from the scientist who, with an array of highly sophisticated instruments, can spot and measure the internal actions of the stress response.

Unfortunately many of the hidden signs outwardly rear their ugly heads only when it is too late. Their continued or frequent action can lead to ill health and death and only then can they be seen! The purpose of being *Stresswise* is to take heed of outward physical and mental signs of stress and to take preventive action before it is too late!

Insight

If you have the physical and mental signs of stress you will also have the hidden signs of increased blood clotting and increased blood glucose and fat levels.

5

Stress and health

In this chapter you will learn:
- *about stress-related disorders and diseases*
- *the ways in which overaction of the stress response can lead to illness*
- *about some proposed mechanisms of prolonged stress effects in immune system suppression and in coronary heart disease.*

> **Insight**
> The stress response involves all body functions, so too much distress overtaxing our adaptive resources can lead to exhaustion, a variety of health problems and can even be fatal.

It has been estimated that at least 75 per cent of illness reported to GPs is stress related. Some doctors have even suggested that almost all illness and premature deaths can be associated with distress. This is not hard to believe when you consider that stress affects all our body systems including our defence and immune mechanisms. We are also more prone to accidents when we are distressed.

Industry and commerce have seen how distress can affect productivity and profits. Surveys and studies have estimated that 100 million working days are lost each year due to distress-related illness and absenteeism, costing the country around £3 billion per annum. Companies pay the price of distress by loss of personnel through resignation or premature retirement. Apart from the personal effects of distress-related ill health, there are also the demands it places on the family. Disability, medical treatment and sick leave from work pose varied and incalculable demands on the family's and nation's caring resources.

***

Insight

Many researchers and doctors now believe that excessive, frequent and/or prolonged action of the stress response, particularly without the normal outlet for the accompanying physical activity, can lead to a variety of disorders and diseases.

***

This is most clearly seen in the cardiovascular system which is heavily involved in the alarm reaction. The digestive system is also very vulnerable. Recent research has shown how cortisol can adversely affect the immune system. Chronic stimulation of this system by cortisol reduces the body's ability to deal with infection and increases susceptibility to diseases such as cancer.

The effects mentioned so far are physical but the emotional disorders, such as anxiety and depression, are perhaps the more obvious consequences of distress. Furthermore, our behaviour and lifestyle frequently change when we are distressed. Altered eating, smoking and drinking patterns and drug abuse bring their own problems and add to the health risks normally associated with these behaviours. Some distress-related disorders and diseases are shown in the list on page 72. These range from symptoms that are simply unpleasant and uncomfortable to more serious illnesses that can be disabling, life-threatening and fatal.

Some distress-related disorders and diseases

Why is it that a response evolved to save life and improve performance ends up actually making us less efficient and becomes a potential killer? To answer this we must go back to many of the points made earlier in Chapter 3. In brief, the stress response was evolved primarily to preserve our lives in the face of life-threatening situations in a physically hostile environment. It was ideal for the threats and challenges faced by our early ancestors, but today we rarely face physical dangers such as an attack by a wild animal. Rather, we live in a society involving complex social interactions. The threats we perceive are to our self-esteem and the security of our relationships and jobs.

Cardiovascular system

Coronary heart disease (angina
  and heart attacks)
Hypertension (high blood
  pressure)
Strokes
Migraine

Digestive system

Indigestion
Nausea
Heartburn
Stomach and duodenal
  ulcers
Ulcerative colitis
Irritable bowel syndrome
Diarrhoea
Constipation
Flatulence

Muscles and joints

Headaches
Cramps
Muscle spasm
Back pain
Neck pain

Others

Diabetes
Cancers
Rheumatoid arthritis
Allergies
Asthma
Common cold and flu
Sexual disorders – reduced sex
  drive, premature ejaculation,
  failure to reach orgasm,
  infertility
Skin disorders
Sleep disorders

Behavioural

Overeating – obesity
Loss of appetite – anorexia
Increased cigarette smoking
Increased caffeine intake
Increased alcohol consumption
Drug abuse

Emotional

Anxiety, including fears,
  phobias and obsessions
Depression

We know Homo sapiens have existed for around 40,000 years in essentially the same biological form as we are today. The urbanized, industrialized, high technology era is a very recent phenomenon in this evolutionary period but has presented the greatest amount of environmental change in a relatively short time. We still have the same biological mechanism – the stress response – to deal with a very different environment. No wonder we suffer the consequences of an outdated biological system which is largely inappropriate for today's demands and pressures.

Today we are bombarded with a continuous stream of emotional threats and challenges and if our beliefs lead us regularly to perceive these as stressors, real or imaginary, then we face the consequences of ill health and death as a result of over-using our stress response.

How the stress response can lead to ill health and death

STRESS RESPONSE AND THE IMMUNE SYSTEM

Insight

One of the most significant effects of long-term stress is the suppression of the immune system brought about by consistently higher than normal levels of cortisol.

Secretion of normal levels of cortisol plays a vital role in helping the body deal with demands and pressure; it helps the body to function at peak performance and to maintain wellbeing. In order to do this, cortisol is secreted in a regular pattern over the course of the day and night (24-hour circadian rhythm); highest levels are secreted in the morning and then the levels decline to the lowest point during late evening to the middle of the night. This pattern of secretion is essential for the normal functioning of the immune system. At night, the cells of the immune system patrol the body, hunting down diseased and damaged cells caused by viral infections and cancerous activity. During the day, the immune system's blood cells, lymphocytes and eosinophils (blood cells which help fight infection), seek out and destroy invading viruses and bacteria, to prevent them from attacking the body cells, tissues and organs. Cortisol helps to orchestrate this switch in immune system activity. However, if the activity of the immune system (particularly the daytime immunity) goes into overdrive, then the cells of the immune system become less effective at carrying out their role. The presence of excessive levels of cortisol can bring about the state of overdrive which is most evident during daytime immunity when we are dealing with pressures and demands.

In excessive amounts, cortisol is known to decrease the number of circulating lymphocytes and eosinophils, cause the thymus and lymph nodes (areas where the lymphocytes are manufactured) to shrivel up, and depress the production of antibodies (agents which fight infection). Thus the immune system is weakened and the ability to fight infection is reduced, so common colds and influenza may be experienced more frequently. In addition, the body can become more susceptible to immune system-related diseases such as rheumatoid arthritis, allergies, skin conditions and asthma. There is also a suggestion that the weakened and less effective immune system can influence the development and recovery of some forms of cancer, however, there is little direct evidence to show that this state can cause cancer.

A frequently reported relationship between stress and the immune system is seen when some individuals take a holiday away from their hectic and demanding jobs. It seems that when the person relaxes their immune system 'relaxes', making them more vulnerable to infections, particularly upper respiratory tract infections.

Furthermore, excessive prolonged periods of exercise, during which there is elevated cortisol secretion, can also trigger upper respiratory tract infections. Many athletes experience this as a result of demanding training regimes leading up to competitions.

THE STRESS RESPONSE, ANGINA AND HEART ATTACKS

> **Insight**
> Excessive levels of noradrenaline can lead to heart and
> circulatory disease, as noradrenaline's most potent action
> is to constrict blood vessels.

During the alarm reaction, this increases the blood pressure, so the
heart must work harder to overcome the higher pressure in order
to circulate the blood. At the same time, noradrenaline steps up
the heart rate, further increasing the heart's workload. A higher
workload requires more oxygen and glucose and this is delivered
to the heart muscles (known as the myocardium) via the coronary
arteries. However, in those people with coronary artery disease*
this could be a problem.

In coronary artery disease, one or more of the coronary arteries
becomes partially obstructed by the build-up of a substance known
as plaque. This furring up is known as atherosclerosis and can lead
to myocardial ischaemia (where the myocardium is poorly supplied
with blood). If a coronary artery becomes severely narrowed,
sufficient blood cannot reach the heart muscle to support its
workload. The resultant myocardial ischaemia produces a pain
across the chest known as angina pectoris. This usually arises
during physical exertion or emotional stress and is relieved by
resting or reducing stress. Those people who suffer from angina
might consider themselves lucky – they have been given a warning
sign that their coronary arteries are becoming progressively and

*It is thought that most people in western societies have some degree of coronary artery
disease. For the majority, this will never cause problems, but others suffer angina or have
a heart attack. Unfortunately it is not easy to predict who is at risk without performing
medical tests. These tests are expensive and carry an element of risk so unless there are
particular medical reasons for doing so, 'healthy' individuals would not be referred for
this investigation. If you have chest pains or are in doubt you should see your doctor.

dangerously narrowed. With the right medication and change in lifestyle, their disease can be managed successfully.

For many, however, the first sign of their coronary artery disease is an unexpected heart attack. Here there is a sudden and severe reduction in the blood supply to the myocardium and part of it dies. If only a small amount of the heart muscle is affected, the victim usually survives and the dead part of the heart turns into a scar. This is usually the case for about half of those who have a heart attack. Their myocardial damage is not extensive enough for complications to arise and serious problems may never occur in the future as long as attention is paid to living a healthy and careful lifestyle. However, for the other half, their heart attack is fatal. In many of these cases a coronary artery is suddenly blocked, leading to cessation of blood supply to the myocardium. This can cause the death of a large part of the heart muscle. Furthermore, the oxygen-starved myocardium can send the heart into ventricular fibrillation (chaotic rapid contractions of the main pumping chambers of the heart) rendering the heart useless as a pump. Under these circumstances, the circulation stops and the victim dies unless the fibrillation is quickly corrected by using a cardiac defibrillator. This device stops the heart beating thus allowing the heart's natural pacemaker to take control again.

Insight

Excessive levels of noradrenaline released during anger and rage could raise the heart's workload to a point where myocardial ischaemia could be fatal. Those people who have angina or have suffered a heart attack are particularly vulnerable.

Noradrenaline can affect its victims in a number of other ways. Some researchers believe that excessive noradrenaline can cause rupture of the plaque, leading to a sudden blockage of the coronary artery. It is thought this occurs because noradrenaline may constrict the small blood vessels that grow into the plaque to provide it with nourishment. Over time, this can lead to plaque necrosis (death of the cells) and eventually plaque rupture. The exposed material of the plaque presents a surface on which a blood clot can form. Clot formation is also encouraged by noradrenaline (remember an action of noradrenaline is to help prevent blood loss if cut during a fight!). The blood supply to the myocardium is suddenly cut off, resulting in a heart attack.

Angina and heart attacks can occur in the absence of significant coronary artery disease. High levels of noradrenaline can cause muscular spasm of the coronary arteries which close up, thereby reducing or stopping blood flow to the myocardium. Excessive levels of noradrenaline and adrenaline are also known to damage the heart muscle cells directly, reducing the contractile ability of the heart. Post-mortem examination of the hearts of patients who have died from a tumour of the adrenal medulla reveals extensive heart muscle damage. This is caused by the extremely high levels of noradrenaline and adrenaline produced by the tumour. Furthermore, excessive catecholamine levels can directly trigger abnormal electrical activity in the heart, resulting in abnormal rhythms which may cause fatal ventricular fibrillation.

STRESS AND SILENT HEART ATTACKS

The development of sophisticated heart monitoring instruments has made it possible to record every heartbeat during a 24-hour period while a person goes about his normal activities. The recordings of the heartbeats, known as the electrocardiogram or ECG for short, are picked up by wires stuck to the chest and recorded on a cassette in a special recorder worn around the waist. The tape is played back through an analyser that detects abnormal rhythms and possible myocardial ischaemia.

We made a 24-hour recording of the heartbeat of a woman taking part in an experiment to investigate factors affecting heart activity. At 8.30 p.m. there was a change in the shape of part of the ECG, known as the ST segment. Changes in this segment usually indicate myocardial ischaemia. The woman had been asked to keep a

24-hour diary of activities and feelings during the experiment, and at around 8.30 p.m. she had recorded a short period of intense emotional arousal soon after she missed her last train home. She reported, 'I was very angry with myself for getting the departure time wrong. I thought it was 8.30, in fact it was 8.15.' The woman had no diagnosed heart disease or any indication of heart problems, yet at 8.30 p.m. a minor myocardial ischaemic episode occurred. What is more, she was completely unaware of it happening and, for this reason, such an attack is known as silent myocardial ischaemia.

Many experiments have used this technique to assess the effect of stress on the heart function of normal healthy individuals and it appears that stress can cause abnormal heart rhythms and myocardial ischaemia severe enough to induce a small silent heart attack!

STRESS, CHOLESTEROL AND HEART DISEASE

Noradrenaline, adrenaline, cortisol and other hormones help mobilize glucose and fats from the body stores, so increasing blood glucose, cholesterol and triglyceride (fat) levels. A high level of circulating blood cholesterol is considered a coronary heart disease risk factor because cholesterol is a major component of plaque. Damage to the inner lining of the blood vessel increases susceptibility to the plaque-forming process by allowing cholesterol to penetrate into the blood vessel wall. There is some evidence to suggest that high circulating levels of noradrenaline and adrenaline can cause this damage.

Insight

It is popularly believed that cholesterol from food is solely responsible for elevating blood cholesterol levels, but it is not always realized that far more is produced during periods of stress than can be obtained from the diet.

A number of research studies have shown how blood cholesterol levels rise during periods of stress. In one such experiment, blood cholesterol was measured in two groups of accountants throughout a period of about six months. During this time, the accountants were asked to keep a record of their lifestyle (diet, exercise and so on) and also how much pressure and stress they experienced. Accountants were chosen for the experiment because they work to deadlines. In fact, one group were tax accountants who had one deadline to meet in April while the others were corporate accountants who had deadlines in January and April. Figure 5.1 shows that, for both groups, there is a peak in blood cholesterol levels coinciding with the deadlines: one for the tax accountants and two for the corporate accountants. Almost all the accountants reported feeling pressured around the time of the deadline but there was no reported significant change in diet or exercise.

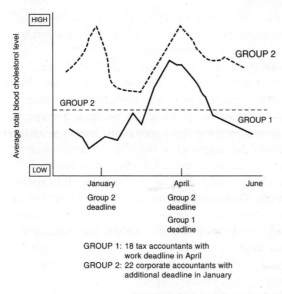

GROUP 1: 18 tax accountants with
work deadline in April
GROUP 2: 22 corporate accountants with
additional deadline in January

adapted from: Friedman & Rosenman Circ. 17.852–861 1958

Figure 5.1 Average blood cholesterol level in accountants as they face deadlines.

When the level of fat in the blood increases, the blood becomes thicker and more viscous. This also occurs when more red cells are pumped into the circulation from the spleen during the stress response. The heart must work harder to circulate thicker blood, therefore myocardial oxygen consumption increases. Another problem with thicker blood is that red blood cells can form a 'sludge' which may block small blood vessels. Sludging in the very small blood vessels of the heart and brain can lead to a heart attack or stroke respectively.

Thus a good case can be made for the involvement of the stress response in circulatory diseases: coronary heart disease, sudden cardiac death, hypertension and strokes. These diseases may result from the interaction between stress and other factors such as diet, smoking and Type A Behaviour.

STRESS RESPONSE AND OTHER DISORDERS AND DISEASES

Eating while the digestive system is partially shut down during stress can lead to a number of problems such as indigestion, nausea and diarrhoea. In addition, many of the body's healing processes are affected. For example, damage to the stomach lining is normally quickly rectified. However, chronic distress slows down the healing process which can lead to prolonged erosion of the wall by acid, increasing the chance of formation of an ulcer due to bacterial or other sources.

The situation is further aggravated because more acid is produced by the stomach during the stress response.

Excessive chronic stress can also lead to weight loss, insomnia, hyperactivity (shakiness and jumpiness) and sexual disorders. Anxiety and fear are often associated with sexual problems: impotence and premature ejaculation in men and difficulty in reaching orgasm in women. Worrying about events, such as job interviews and examinations, can lead to menstrual cycle irregularities, loss of interest in sexual activities and reduced fertility. Emotional factors are thought to account for around 25 per cent of all infertility problems.

Persistently high blood sugar levels can occur during prolonged distress, leading to diabetes. The depletion of endorphins (pain suppressors) during chronic stress makes pain more apparent in diseases such as arthritis. Back and neck pain, headaches and migraines, brought on by prolonged muscle tension during the stress response are less bearable. Chronic distress can also lead to severe anxiety and depression, disabling mental illnesses, nervous breakdown and suicide.

6

Stress and performance

In this chapter you will learn:
- *that stress can lead to underperformance*
- *that stress can lead to peak performance*
- *how stress can result in burn-out.*

Life would be dull and uninteresting if we did not experience
the stimulating feeling of eustress associated with the challenge
of physical performance and the testing of our skills and mental
ability. In this case, the effects of a challenge will not usually
lead to ill health, provided the energy generated by the stress
response is used appropriately and we feel in control and able
to cope. However, too few demands or excessive demands (either
one major or several minor demands) can overtax our ability
to cope effectively, even in those who have good coping ability.
This is particularly so if these demands occur frequently or are
prolonged. The effect of stress on performance is illustrated in
Figure 6.1.

The performance curve

Too little stimulation, too few demands and challenges can lead
to boredom, frustration and a feeling that we are not using our
abilities to the full. This situation will tip the stress balance into the
distress zone and result in poor performance in whatever we do.

Similarly, excessive demands can be very distressful, for example, work overload, extreme time pressure, inescapable demands imposed by others, and too many stressful life events. Such demands can make us feel that control is slipping away, we start doubting our ability to cope and consequently our performance suffers. This is particularly so where the tasks are complicated, unusual or unfamiliar. On the other hand, where we perceive demands and challenges as well within our capabilities and we feel confident in handling the task, then performance improves and reaches a peak. However, even those who usually cope well will inevitably suffer some reduction of performance when they are under extreme pressure and dealing with excessive demands. Too much effort and trying too hard often fails to achieve the desired result. Working flat out under high pressure (that is, many demands) to get things done is not always the right strategy, as can be seen in Figure 6.1. This way of working may achieve goals in the short term, but working at high pressure over a long period will inevitably take its toll on the performance, productivity, relationships and health of most people.

Working in this way is like running a car without stopping to service it. As long as the tank is filled with petrol, the engine will keep running, but what happens when the tyres lose air and the spark plugs are not changed? Performance drops. Eventually, if the car continues to be driven without any attention, it will break down.

Some people can successfully concentrate a high workload into a short period and achieve effective results but they know when to stop for a break. They take the necessary time to relax and recharge their batteries.

PEAK PERFORMANCE

Maximum performance is achieved on the top part of the upward slope of the performance curve where we feel stimulated, alert, are better at making decisions, are more creative and effective in achieving results.

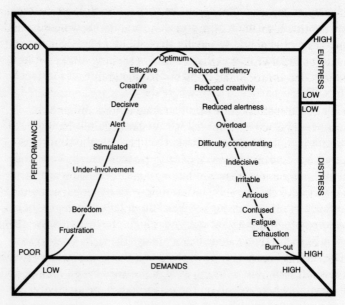

Figure 6.1 Stress and performance.

Insight

Peak performance is reached when we are dealing with just the right number and type of demands and challenges and we feel confident and well able to handle them.

ON THE SLIPPERY SLOPE TO DISASTER

However, if demands and pressures continue to increase beyond this point, our coping resources become steadily overtaxed and our performance starts to decline. We hit the downward slope of the curve. If this continues, then we could find ourselves on the slippery slope of the distress zone: experiencing anxiety, fatigue, exhaustion and mental breakdown, often referred to as 'burn-out'.

NORADRENALINE AND ADRENALINE AGAIN

Looking back at the actions of the stress response and the effects of noradrenaline and adrenaline, it is clear to see how stress affects performance. Noradrenaline increases alertness, improves concentration, mental ability, learning and decision-making and it makes us feel good. Adrenaline has none of these benefits and makes us feel awful. It can make us forget things more easily, reduce concentration and decision-making ability.

Being in the eustress zone means having a predominance of noradrenaline activity. But do not be alarmed after having read about how noradrenaline can lead to ill health and death! Being in the eustress zone means activating the stress response by just the right amount so that you feel confident in dealing with your demands and challenges. The amount of noradrenaline released in the body to achieve this is not harmful. It is only when excessive amounts of noradrenaline are released that harm may arise. This can occur when too much eustress is experienced. Too many eustressful demands can overtax the body in a similar way to many distressful demands. You can have too much of a good thing!

The effect of stress on industry, commerce and the professions

The costs of distress in terms of health, performance and productivity are all too clear for the individual, but the cost to organizations, industry, commerce and the professions is often not appreciated. Considerable financial losses can result from absenteeism due to stress-related disorders and loss of trained personnel through early retirement or premature death. But these calculable costs represent only the tip of a huge financial iceberg. What is difficult to estimate is the cost of distress hidden 'below the waterline' (see Figure 6.2).

Furthermore, individuals in the distress zone are more accident-prone. Someone might, for example, be worried about finding the money to pay a pile of domestic bills. With his mind obsessed by this problem, concentration wanders from the task in hand with the chance that a wrong button may be pushed!

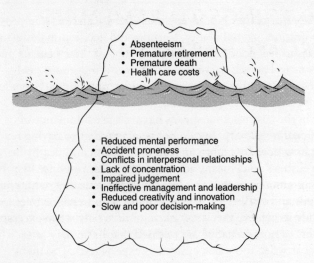

- Absenteeism
- Premature retirement
- Premature death
- Health care costs

- Reduced mental performance
- Accident proneness
- Conflicts in interpersonal relationships
- Lack of concentration
- Impaired judgement
- Ineffective management and leadership
- Reduced creativity and innovation
- Slow and poor decision-making

Figure 6.2 The stress iceberg.

An organization's greatest asset is its employees – it is their mental as well as physical health, wellbeing, morale and productivity that is revealed in the balance sheets. It makes sense for companies and organizations to consider that good mental and physical health is good business.

Employers can provide training and development programmes and create the right environment and atmosphere for their employees to work in the eustress zone and away from the distress zone. Ultimately, however, it is only the employees themselves who can take the steps to enter the eustress zone and keep the distress zone at bay. This involves all aspects of their lives – at home and with friends as well as at work. Identifying the sources of stress will help in taking these steps.

10 THINGS TO REMEMBER FROM CHAPTERS 4, 5 AND 6

1 *The ability to recognize and monitor the signs and symptoms of the stress response is a crucial skill in managing stress.*

2 *Learn to listen to your body; read and take note of the messages it is sending to you.*

3 *Signs and symptoms are a result of the action of noradrenaline (preparing the body for fighting and aggression), adrenaline (preparing the body for a quick getaway) and cortisol (preparing the body to deal with long term demands).*

4 *Being alert to the signs of distress in others will help you to reduce relationship problems and to maintain a creative and productive office and organization.*

5 *Do not forget that there are signs and symptoms that cannot be seen.*

6 *Excessive frequent and/or action of the stress response can lead to a variety of disorders and diseases and can be fatal.*

7 *Long-term stress suppresses the immune system.*

8 *Excessive levels of noradrenaline are released during anger, and rage raises the heart workload and increases blood clotting, both of which can be fatal in those at risk from a heart attack.*

9 *Blood cholesterol is elevated more by what happens inside you as a result of long-term stress, rather than what you put into your mouth.*

10 *Visualize the stress performance curve. Peak performance is achieved when we are dealing well with the right number of demands and challenges.*

7

Sources of stress

In this chapter you will learn:
- *about factors that can trigger the stress response*
- *about Type A Behaviour and generating avoidable stress*
- *about life events and unavoidable stress.*

> **Insight**
> Stress is an inevitable part of our existence.

Everything in our environment can be a potential source of stress, but ultimately *stress comes from within you*; it is a result of how you perceive the situations and events in your environment. The way you perceive these situations depends to a great extent on your beliefs and attitudes. Some people have beliefs that lead them to perceive situations as threatening and challenging when in fact no real threat or challenge exists. As a result, these people, called 'Type As', generate unnecessary stress for themselves. This stress can be avoided by modifying beliefs and habits. On the other hand, some events during our lives will almost certainly be stressful. These are referred to as 'life events'; they are mostly unavoidable and we have to adapt or readjust our lives to cope with them.

> **Insight**
> We are most likely to experience stress in our relationships with others, particularly at work and at home.

Much of this stress is associated with threats and challenges to our self-esteem and self-image, the security and stability of our jobs and family relationships.

The nature of the demands

Anything in the environment that leads to activation of the stress response is termed a 'stressor'. Your view of the environment and how you interact with it will determine whether or not the object or event becomes a stressor for you. However, there are some physical stressors that are clearly life-threatening and we would all see them as such. We see that we are in danger with little time to plan our action, so our alarm response is quickly summoned. Most of us also treat novel and unusual situations as stressors, since we have no past experience in dealing with them. For these and other stressors, the amount and type of stress experienced and the activity level of the stress response depends on how we perceive the nature of the demand or threat. How important is it to us, how long does it last, how often does it occur and how clear are we about what is happening? To illustrate the nature of the demands, we can use the example of being held up in heavy traffic. This considers the 'on your marks' part of the stress response sequence described on page 35.

IMPORTANCE OF THE STRESSOR

Some people do not mind being held up in heavy, slow-moving traffic since losing some time is of no importance to them. On the other hand others 'tear their hair out' because the delay will make them late for an important meeting. They may become angry and hostile towards other drivers, especially those jumping the queue. The point is that the importance of the stressor to you will determine the degree to which your stress response is activated.

DURATION OF THE STRESSOR

Being held up in a traffic jam for a few minutes may cause some irritation in a driver who is late for a meeting but if the traffic jam persists, he may 'blow a fuse'. How long each stressor lasts will affect your stress balance and the extent to which your stress response is activated. Some stressors last a short time, such as a job interview, while others persist for long periods, for example, dealing with relationship difficulties.

INTENSITY OF THE STRESSOR

Our delayed driver will probably react less strongly to a queue of ten cars ahead than he would to a queue of 100 cars stretching into the distance.

FREQUENCY OF THE STRESSOR

Getting out of one traffic jam only to find himself in another can keep our driver's fuse smouldering. He may meet unexpected traffic hold-ups every day while commuting: a car broken down, an accident or a lorry shedding its load. How often stressors occur will determine where your stress balance lies and to what extent your stress response is activated.

UNCERTAINTY ABOUT THE STRESSOR

As our delayed driver approaches the traffic jam he may immediately treat it as a stressor because he is uncertain how long he will be delayed. 'How far does this hold-up go on for?' he mutters to himself as he views the line of traffic disappearing round the next bend. 'What will happen if I'm late for my meeting?' For many of us, worrying about what is *likely* to happen is a major source of distress.

Type A Behaviour

In the mid 1950s, two American cardiologists investigated the possible role of emotional stress in bringing on a heart attack. They asked several hundred industrialists and 100 doctors treating coronary patients, 'What do you think caused the heart attack of a friend or patient?' The majority said stress. The pressure to meet deadlines and excessive competition were singled out as the main culprits. Fascinated by the fact that emotional stress might play a role in coronary heart disease, these two cardiologists started to look at their own patients in a different way. As well as taking blood pressure and assessing cholesterol levels, they looked for signs of emotional stress. It soon emerged that many of their coronary patients behaved in a similar way. Body movements and speech characteristics, as well as what the patients said during consultations, painted the same picture of individuals who were rushed, impatient, excessively competitive, ambitious and easily irritated. These early observations of what became known as Type A Behaviour formed the basis of much research investigating the link between emotional stress and heart disease.

So what exactly is Type A Behaviour? We described earlier how much of the way in which we interpret situations depends on our beliefs, attitudes and expectations.

Insight

Type A individuals have beliefs, attitudes and expectations that engage them in a constant struggle to gain control over their environment.

Type A people battle vigorously to achieve and maintain control, and when they sense this is being challenged or threatened, they respond by behaving in a Type A manner. Each time Type As perceive such emotional threats and challenges, they *automatically* trigger their stress response. But there is no *real* threat or challenge to their life. As a result, they generate much unnecessary stress for themselves which keeps them frequently outside the normal zone of the stress balance and in the distress zone. Traffic jams, queues at the supermarket and bank, and finding the toothpaste squeezed from the middle of the tube are examples of situations, that Type As find threatening. So in response to these situations, their heart rate accelerates and pounds, their blood clots more easily and cholesterol levels rise – all for no purpose. With his body prepared for physical action by activation of the stress response, the Type A individual can only sit and fume in his car. He cannot get out and run up and down the traffic lanes or abandon his car and run away; nor can he engage in a fight with other motorists.

To be *Stresswise*, you need to identify Type A Behaviour in yourself so that you can take steps to reduce and modify it. This is possible because Type A Behaviour is primarily a learned way of interacting with the environment. Type A Behaviour is chiefly identified by a constant sense of time urgency and easily aroused irritation and aggravation. It is observed in an individual who tries to do more and more in less and less time, thinks about or does two or more things simultaneously, and frequently becomes angry in response to trivial happenings.

Type As might be described as agitated, hard-driving, hasty, hostile, hurried, impatient and irritable. They are often poor listeners, rushed, over-competitive and over-ambitious. People who have very few of these characteristics are described as Type B. They are calm, content, controlled, easy-going, good listeners, not easily irritated, patient and unhurried.

The assessment you completed at the beginning of this book will give you an idea of your self-perceived level of Type A Behaviour. The questionnaire below will provide a more accurate measure of this. For each question tick the box that best represents your behaviour.

TYPE A BEHAVIOUR

For each question, tick the box that best represents your behaviour.

	Never	Almost never	Some-times	Usually	Almost always	Always
Are you late for appointments?	☐	☐	☐	☐	☐	☐
Are you competitive in the games you play at home or at work?	☐	☐	☐	☐	☐	☐
In conversations, do you anticipate what others are going to say (head nod, interrupt, finish sentences for them)?	☐	☐	☐	☐	☐	☐

	Never	Almost never	Some- times	Usually	Almost always	Always
Do you have to do things in a hurry?	❑	❑	❑	❑	❑	❑
Do you get impatient in queues or traffic jams?	❑	❑	❑	❑	❑	❑
Do you try to do several things at once and think about what you are about to do next?	❑	❑	❑	❑	❑	❑
Do you feel you do most things quickly (eating, walking, talking, driving)?	❑	❑	❑	❑	❑	❑
Do you get easily irritated over trivia?	❑	❑	❑	❑	❑	❑
If you make a mistake, do you get angry with yourself?	❑	❑	❑	❑	❑	❑
Do you find fault with and criticize other people?	❑	❑	❑	❑	❑	❑
Total						

For scoring and evaluation turn to page 225. When you have calculated your score write this in the box on page 114.

You should note that this is a self-assessment of your Type A Behaviour. It is only as accurate as you are honest in your answers. Furthermore, Type As are often blind to their own behaviour for example, doing things fast. Type As may not think they are as fast as they actually are.

The questionnaire is based on some common Type A characteristics, many of which are simple to detect, while others are subtle and not so obviously related to time urgency and easily aroused anger and hostility. If a person possesses a large number of Type A characteristics and displays these frequently and excessively, then he is considered to be an extreme Type A. On a scale of 0–100, the spectrum of Type A Behaviour ranges from mild (score 40–59 per cent) and moderate (score 60–79 per cent) to severe (score 80–100 per cent), with Type B individuals described as having very few Type A characteristics (score less than 39 per cent). Using a similar questionnaire, we have surveyed over 5,000 people and found that only 10 per cent were Type B, 80 per cent mild–moderate Type A and 10 per cent extreme Type A.

IDENTIFYING TYPE A BEHAVIOUR

To help you identify Type A Behaviour, we will describe some typical and some extreme examples.

In an attempt to gain control, Type As become 'hurry sick'; they adopt two strategies with which to save time to get more and more done in less and less time. Firstly, they practise 'speedup' – doing things fast to save time. So they eat fast, walk fast, drive fast and talk fast. Some Type As take 'speedup' to extremes. Type A men have admitted to shaving with two electric razors at once, to save time! On hearing this, a woman reporter admitted to us that she blow-dries her hair with two hairdryers at the same time. But incredible though these actions may seem to Type Bs, and also to many Type As for that matter, they are insignificant when compared to the man who liquidizes all his meals so he can drink them to save time!

Not content with the amount of time saved by 'speedup', Type As turn to 'polyphasing' – doing two or more things at the same time. So they clean their teeth or shave while taking a shower, or continue writing a document while engaged in a telephone conversation on a completely different subject. As they drive to work, Type As shave, apply make-up, eat breakfast or read the morning paper. Extreme Type As regard it as a challenge to see how many different things they can do at the same time. We heard of a businessman in San Francisco who installed a hinged desktop in his toilet so that he could continue working while attending to the call of nature. By now he may well have a fax machine installed in the 'smallest room' and have acquired a headset telephone to leave his hands free. There may be some sense in his actions because many extreme Type As often ignore the calls of nature until the last minute and frequently suffer from constipation, which then makes them annoyed at the time they waste in the toilet!

Insight

Neuroscientists believe that our brains get log-jammed with nerve messages when we try to do more than one thing at a time. As a result, if we try to multitask, then we are more likely to make mistakes, under-perform and put ourselves and others in danger, such as while driving.

Wasting time in queues is something Type As cannot tolerate. They will seek ways in which to beat, jump or avoid queuing at the bank, post office, shops, garage, traffic lights and so on. Take the supermarket situation and an extreme Type A shopper coming up to the checkouts. While nobody would choose to join the longest queue, our extreme Type A shopper will make several decisions before selecting a queue. First, Type As count the number of people in the queue then multiply this by the number of items in each basket and trolley. Many of us may well do this, but Type As will go further. They assess the efficiency of the checkout operator before making their choice of which queue to join. A decision is made and the 'fastest' queue joined. Now, instead of simply queuing, Type As take other people as markers in other queues to see if they have made the right choice. Noradrenaline levels start to rise when our Type A realizes that the markers are making better progress – 'Why do I always choose the wrong queue?', our Type A curses. Noradrenaline levels then hit the roof when the person in front of their queue holds them up by paying by credit card or cheque, and sky-high levels are reached when they get to the checkout and the till roll runs out. Our Type A finally leaves the store angry at himself and quick to vent this anger on others. Learning from this situation, Type As have adopted several strategies to beat the supermarket queue. One Type A proudly described how he took six trolleys and put five items in each and went through the express checkout six times!

TYPE A BEHAVIOUR AND HOSTILITY

The supermarket battleground may give rise to a few confrontations with other shoppers, but impatience in the driving situation exposes the ugly side of extreme Type A Behaviour. The typical Type A driver will always strive to drive as fast as possible, jump the red light and make Grand Prix starts just as the lights turn green. They relentlessly and obsessively drive close to the car in front and overtake at any possible, or even near-impossible, opportunity. They will compulsively switch lanes in traffic jams and take alternative routes in an attempt to avoid an apparent hold-up, often not knowing exactly where they are heading!

One extreme Type A recalled how he fought a constant stress battle always to avoid any lane which might be bottled up. 'If I see a slow-moving car or lorry I'm out of its way before I'm anywhere near to it,' he exclaimed. In fact, he admitted that his driving behaviour in this respect was so successful that he usually arrived early for his appointments and had to sit in his car and wait!

A participant at one of our workshops told us of his experience when being driven to a meeting by a work colleague. 'My colleague's driving was so Type A. He would shout at other drivers who got in his way, he would even wind the window down to get more effect, flash his lights and sound the horn. I swear I'm not going with him again if he drives.' A week later another meeting came up and our participant insisted that he drove instead of his Type A colleague. 'You wouldn't believe it,' he told us. 'My colleague flashed *my* lights and wound *my* window down and *shouted at me* to do the same!'

Such driving behaviour seems harmless when compared to that of some Californian drivers who have shot dead or wounded other motorists who annoyed them. Sadly, there are many examples of road rage in Britain. Recently on the M4, a driver was forced to stop, and was then assaulted by a motorist who had been attempting to overtake. Another motorist met his fate at the end of a tyre mallet when he angered the driver behind by allowing a woman with a pram to cross at the lights when they turned to green. Then there is the car-park space – scene of many aggressive confrontations as two drivers aim for the only vacant spot. Similar barrages of abuse fill the air when a passing place is too narrow and both drivers feel the other should reverse.

Being held up, thus having valuable time taken away from them, makes Type As angry and hostile. This reflects the general tendency for Type As to be very easily irritated and angry over trivial happenings and the mistakes of others and themselves. They can blow a fuse when they find the toothpaste squeezed from the middle of the tube if they always methodically squeeze it from the bottom. In America, we heard of a heart attack patient whose wife had put the toilet roll on the holder the wrong way round. The husband grabbed the roll, confronted his wife with it and screamed at her, 'How many times have I told you to...' He had a second, non-fatal heart attack. We hear you ask yourself which way round did this man like his toilet roll? There is only one right way, as you know – with the paper coming over the top, of course. Well, it has to be according to the man because, 'You wouldn't see the pattern if the paper hung over the back.' That highlights another Type A characteristic – they think they are always right.

Insight
Irritation, anger and hostility generated and aimed at others harms the very person we least expect it to – ourselves.

The noradrenaline released in this situation can be a killer! So the message is *do not get mad in the first place; modify your beliefs and attitudes to reduce this inappropriate Type A Behaviour.* How to do this is the topic of Chapter 13.

Sometimes it is difficult to understand why such trivial things lead Type As into the countdown for blast-off. One participant working with a group to modify his Type A Behaviour would regularly recall at meetings how cutting his lawn caused him much aggravation. His wife described how she heard a noise coming from the garden and found her husband smashing the electric mower against the concrete washing-line post. With bits of mower strewn around the garden, he shouted, 'B... thing keeps cutting out!' His wife pointed out that he had only bought it two weeks ago and it was still under guarantee! With such behaviour over cutting the lawn, we pictured the garden as having half an acre or so of grass. It was in fact only a few square metres!

By describing Type A Behaviour in this way, we hope to give you a guide to identifying it in yourself and others. Type As tend to be excessively competitive, ambitious and self-involved. They are poor listeners, interrupt while others are talking, head-nod to encourage the speaker to hurry along and often bring the conversation around to themselves. In conversations they frequently self-reference, that is, they often refer to themselves by regular use of pronouns 'I', 'me', 'my' and 'mine'. They frequently describe things in unnecessary detail, are obsessed with numbers and quantities and with their achievements at work and in everything they do.

TYPE A WORKAHOLICS

We asked a Type A doctor to describe her life briefly. She replied, 'I was the youngest consultant appointed at [ ] Hospital, I have a thriving private practice, I have published 120 scientific articles and lectured around the world...'. When she had finished, we said, 'But earlier you mentioned you were married with children but you never referred to this once'. In fact, we discovered that this doctor works so much that she moved her word processor into the lounge to be with her husband.

Type As find it difficult to believe that their way of behaving is counter-productive. Type Bs give themselves more time and space to be creative and are more effective in the long run, often advancing their careers!

Insight
Contrary to popular belief, Type Bs are also ambitious and competitive people, but they go about things in a different way.

As a result, they achieve their goals without suffering ill health. They usually have more fulfilling family relationships and a good social life.

Type A Behaviour is conducive to workaholism. Workaholics invariably suffer marital and social relationship problems, as they struggle for success and need to work longer and longer hours to achieve their goals. This clearly spells distress. You can assess whether or not you are a workaholic by completing the questionnaire below.

YOUR ATTITUDE TO WORK – WORKAHOLISM

	Yes	No
Do you take work home most nights?	❑	❑
Do you frequently think about work problems at home?	❑	❑
Do you voluntarily work long hours?	❑	❑
Do work problems affect your sleeping habits?	❑	❑
Do your family and friends complain that you spend too little time with them?	❑	❑
Do you find it difficult to relax and forget work?	❑	❑
Do you find it difficult to say 'no' to work requests?	❑	❑
Do you find it difficult to delegate?	❑	❑
Is your self-esteem based largely on your work?	❑	❑
Score		

Turn to page 226 for scoring and evaluation. Write your score in the box on page 114.

A woman told us how her workaholic husband cancelled a week of their fortnight's family self-catering holiday because of work commitments. She then described what happened: 'We set off for Cornwall via his office and waited in the car park for nearly two hours. On the Tuesday evening he said he had arranged a business appointment for the following day. He arrived back in Cornwall in the early hours of Thursday morning. On the way home from holiday he insisted on calling in at his office again. This time we waited just over an hour. This isn't the first time a holiday has gone like this. We are never going on holiday with him again!'

Frequently, Type As find it difficult to relax and switch off from work. They are the people who come back from the Costa del Sol with three white lines across their forehead or who telephone the office every day or pack business work in their suitcase. Often they feel obliged to take work home and are only happy if their briefcases are bulging at the seams!

Type As will often say, 'I thrive on stress'. In fact, what they are saying is, 'I am addicted to noradrenaline'. This addiction produces a feeling of confidence and elation and often leads Type As to seek out challenging situations to keep their noradrenaline levels high.

Are you addicted to noradrenaline?
Signs of noradrenaline addiction:

- *Mind frequently racing*
- *Difficulty in getting to sleep*
- *Smoking too much*
- *Drinking too much caffeine*
- *Hyperactive.*

TYPE A BEHAVIOUR AND HEALTH

Excessive, frequent and prolonged release of noradrenaline is thought to increase the risk of heart disease, high blood pressure, migraine and ulcers. Type As usually over-react to challenges and threats and, faced with a demanding situation, they over-activate their sympathetic nervous system, releasing much noradrenaline. The dangers of this were outlined in Chapter 5.

Unfortunately, self-induced stress in Type As often distorts their perception and they fail to recognize what is happening to them.

However, not all Type As succumb to the ill effects of stress. It has been suggested that a personality factor described as 'hardiness' (stress resistance) interacts with Type A Behaviour to minimize its risk to health. Hardy people look upon situations as challenges rather than threats. They have commitment to what they do and feel confident about gaining control. They turn stressful life events into possibilities or opportunities for personal growth and benefit. More research is needed in this area to clarify the involvement of hardiness with stress and health.

The stress generated by Type A Behaviour is avoidable by modifying beliefs, attitudes and habits. This is dealt with in Chapter 13.

Life events

Some stressors are unavoidable and will affect most of us at some time during our lives. These are often referred to as 'life events' and are crises that must be faced, for example, illness and injury to yourself, family and friends, and bereavement. Other crises may occur, such as marital disharmony, problems with children, financial difficulties and work problems. There are also events that require some adjustment on our part, such as moving to a new house, changing jobs, children starting school. Our stress response is activated to help us deal with these changes, events and crises.

Insight
Research has shown that if we experience too many life events during a short period, our adaptive and coping resources may be overtaxed and this can lead to ill health.

Complete the questionnaire on the next page to assess whether your life events are putting you at a higher risk of ill health.

The life events scale was developed by researchers in the United States while undertaking a study to establish which events occurring during a person's life required the most readjustment. Forty-three life events making up the questionnaire were selected as being the most common and stressful. You will notice that some events, such as illness and bereavement, are traumatic and likely to give rise to distress whereas others, such as marriage, birth of a child or moving house, might be expected to be pleasant and enjoyable experiences. However, they all require a change in the person's life as they readjust to the new situation. You will see on page 227 that each event is given a score on a scale from 0 to 100. The scores are based on how much adjustment people felt they needed to make in order to cope with each situation, if getting married is rated at 50 points. As expected, most people rated death of a spouse at the maximum score of 100, while at the other end of the scale, Christmas was valued at 12 and minor violations of the law, 11. Subsequent research using this scale showed that those people who scored over 100 points in their previous year had an increased risk of suffering a major illness during the next two years.

Even though these types of stressor are unavoidable, our beliefs and attitudes can play a major part in how we perceive them and how much stress, if any, we experience. For example, bereavement is undoubtedly a major stressor, but our religious beliefs may reduce the stress experienced.

LIFE EVENTS

Tick off the listed events which you have experienced during the last 12 months, then turn to page 227 to check your list against the scores for each item. Write your score in the box for each item and then add up the scores. Write your total score in the box on page 114.

	TICK	SCORE			TICK	SCORE
Death of a partner	☐	___	Child leaves home		☐	___
Divorce	☐	___	Trouble with in-laws		☐	___
Separation from partner	☐	___	Outstanding personal achievement		☐	___
Jail sentence	☐					
Death of a close family member	☐	___	Partner begins or stops work		☐	___
			Child begins or ends school		☐	___
Injury or illness to yourself	☐	___	Change in living conditions		☐	___
Marriage – your own	☐	___	Change of personal habits		☐	___
Given the sack at work	☐	___	Trouble with boss or employer		☐	
Reconciliation with partner	☐	___	Change in working hours and conditions		☐	___
Retirement	☐	___	Change in residence		☐	___
Ill health in member of family	☐	___	Child changes schools		☐	___
Pregnancy – your own	☐	___	Change in recreation		☐	___
Sexual problems/difficulties	☐	___	Change in church activities		☐	___
Addition of new family member	☐	___	Change in social activities		☐	___
Major business or work changes	☐	___	Take on a small mortgage or loan		☐	___
			Change in sleeping habits		☐	___
Change in your financial state	☐	___	Change in number of family get-togethers		☐	___
Death of a friend	☐	___				
Change to a different type of work	☐	___	Change in eating habits		☐	___
			Holiday		☐	___
More arguments with partner	☐	___	Christmas (coming soon)		☐	___
Take on a large mortgage	☐	___	Minor violations of the law		☐	___
Mortgage or loan foreclosed	☐	___				
Change in responsibilities at work	☐	___	TOTAL SCORE			☐

This scale is adapted from Holmes and Rahe's Life Change Index, *Journal of Psychosomatic Research*, 1967 Vol. 11.

Family, social and work situations

We spend about a third of our life at work, a further third sleeping and the remaining third with our family and friends. Many people find that the most distress in their lives arises from relationships with others, both in the family and social setting, and at work. Look back at the life events list and you will see how many are associated with relationships for example, marital disharmony, problems with children, problems with neighbours, problems with the boss or co-workers. Similarly, there are a number of events relating to work. Work is commonly cited as a major cause of distress and there are many reasons for this, for example:

- ▶ *work overload – simply having too much to do*
- ▶ *time pressures and impossible deadlines to meet*
- ▶ *how well and to what extent you feel your skills and abilities are being used*
- ▶ *poorly defined or understood job role*
- ▶ *changes in procedures*
- ▶ *poor communication – not knowing what is going on and not feeling part of the organization.*

Sometimes these demands may be imposed on you by others and you feel pressured and not in control. Use the 'Identifying stress at work' questionnaire on page 106 to assess your level of job satisfaction. Being dissatisfied with a particular aspect of your job may not mean you find it stressful so you should also rate your perceived stress experience for each item.

There is no scoring system for this checklist but carrying out this exercise will help you to focus on those aspects at work which may be sources of stress for you. This is a first step for dealing with stress at work. Using the coping strategies described in Part three, you should be able to find ways of resolving problems.

Work stress can also be self-imposed, for example, setting unrealistic goals, attempting to change too much too quickly. You may need to stand back and ask yourself how your stress is arising.

Are you asking too much of people who work for you? Are you creating unnecessary stress for yourself? Are you a workaholic?

It may be that you regard your stress as being derived only from work or home but usually it is from both. Stress from family arguments or financial worries can affect our work performance; our minds might not be on the job at hand and accidents or mistakes can easily occur. Feeling generally distressed will make us less able to handle the inevitable pressures and demands of our job. On the other hand, a happy home life with few major worries can help us ride through the pressures of work without distress. Similarly, a day at work full of pressure, demands and situations that lower our self-esteem can continue when we get home. Then it takes just a minor irritation to make us snap at our partner or shout at the children.

Often before we realize what is happening, we can enter into a vicious circle and things can go from bad to worse. So stress must be tackled throughout all aspects of our lives. This is what the *Stresswise* programme is about – learning to deal with stress and to care for yourself and your relationships.

Insight

We should remember that family, social and work situations can be a source of much joy, love, support and stimulation.

They can provide security and self-esteem. Building on these can keep you away from the distress zone and direct you into the eustress zone.

Please turn the page and complete the Identifying stress at work questionnaire.

IDENTIFYING STRESS AT WORK

This questionnaire is a guide to help identify stressors at work. For each aspect of your job write the stress rating to indicate how much stress you experience. Add your scores and write the total in the box. For scoring and evaluation please turn to page 228.

Stress rating
0 = no stress
1 = slightly stressful
2 = moderately stressful
3 = very stressful
4 = extremely stressful

Aspects of your job	Stress rating
The physical conditions at work, e.g. ventilation, noise, lighting, heating	☐
The freedom to choose your work	☐
The freedom to get on with your work your colleagues	☐
The recognition you get for good work	☐
Having more than one immediate boss	☐
Your immediate boss or bosses	☐
The amount of responsibility you are given	☐
Your rate of pay	☐
Your opportunity to use your abilities	☐
Industrial relations between management and workers in your organization	☐
Your chance of promotion	☐
The way your organization is managed	☐
The attention paid to suggestions you make	☐
The number of hours worked	☐
The amount of variety in your job	☐
The security of your employment	☐
Any other aspects	☐
Total score	☐

10 THINGS TO REMEMBER FROM CHAPTER 7

1 *Everything in our environment can be a potential source of stress, but ultimately stress comes from within us.*

2 *Most stress is experienced in our relationships with others at home and at work.*

3 *The stress we experience depends on the importance of the stressor to us, how long it lasts, how intense and frequent it is, and how uncertain we are about it.*

4 *Some individuals, known as Type As, through their beliefs, attitudes and expectations, activate their stress response when no real threat or challenge exists.*

5 *Anger and hostility aimed at others harms you more than the person you are confronting.*

6 *Type Bs are as ambitious and competitive as Type As, however, they achieve their goals without suffering the ill health often experienced by Type As.*

7 *If we experience too many life events in a short period, our adaptive and coping responses may be overtaxed and this increases our chances of suffering ill health.*

8 *The higher your life event score, the more you will be risk of ill health.*

9 *Stress at work will affect your life at home and stress at home will affect your performance at work.*

10 *Nurture relationships with others. Good supportive relationships will improve your self-esteem which will help you to deal with your demands and pressures.*

Part three

Dealing with stress

8

Personal stress management
planning: preparation

In this chapter you will learn:
- *how to devise a personal, practical stress management plan*
- *how to monitor signs and symptoms for stress management*
- *how to assess key stressors for stress management planning.*

Dealing with stress involves *short-term* 'fire-fighting' by knowing what to do in the event of a stressor occurring acutely, and *long-term* prevention by adopting a lifestyle that will minimize stress. In both cases, you need to have the knowledge and/or experience to draw upon, in order to cope with stress. There are many techniques for dealing with stress. The more techniques you know about, the more able you will be to deal with stress effectively. You will have a greater appreciation of what techniques are appropriate to deal with a particular stressor. Practising a variety of techniques will build up experience needed to tackle stress in the long term. Planning what to do in advance can reduce potential distress.

Insight

Practising a stress management plan may enable you to avoid potential stressors.

This preventative approach is the essence of effective stress management.

In this chapter you will be guided on *how to prepare for a plan* to manage your stress: your *stress management plan*. This plan, described in Chapter 15, is designed as a 12-week programme to deal with stressors in your life, using a variety of stress management techniques described in Chapters 9 to 14.

Summary of self-assessment

Having worked through Part two of this book and completed the questionnaires, you may find it helpful to summarize the results of your self-assessments as a starting point for your stress management plan.

SIGNS AND SYMPTOMS

From your signs and symptoms questionnaire on pages 61–2, write the score in Figure 8.1 opposite. Then identify your three highest scoring signs and symptoms and write these in the table.

Identifying the key signs and symptoms arising from the activity of your stress response will help you to monitor your reaction to the demands and pressures you encounter. These signs and symptoms will be an indicator of your ability to cope. Use these as a means of reflecting on what may be causing stress for you.

Monitoring your signs and symptoms can also provide you with a guide to show how effective your strategies are for dealing with stress. Reassessing your signs and symptoms can provide a useful stress level check for you, as described in Chapter 15.

Managing stress is a dynamic process since demands and pressures are continually changing. A good starting point for developing your personal stress management plan is to review your current situation by identifying your most significant stressors. Do this by looking back at the questionnaires you have completed, note the score and select *three* significant items from each questionnaire, as indicated in Figure 8.2 (page 114).

Date:	
Signs and symptoms score:	

Key signs and symptoms:

My three highest scoring signs and symptoms:	1	
	2	
	3	

Figure 8.1 Summary of my signs and symptoms of self-assessment.

Now identify your top *three* overall most significant stressors. From the summary of stressors that you have listed in Figure 8.2, identify the *three stressors* that you consider to be your key *stressors*. List these in Figure 8.3 (page 114).

Your stress management plan (SMP) is designed as a 12-week programme to deal with three key stressors in your life. A week-by-week guide, which shows you how to work out and implement an SMP and how to assess your progress, is provided in Chapter 15. You may well identify several stressors you wish to deal with, however, to tackle stress effectively it is helpful to concentrate on dealing with two or three demands at a time.

It is also important for you to recognize that your stressors could, in fact, be due to your appraisal or perception of a situation. It may well turn out that through the SMP, you will use techniques to change your view of how you see your circumstances. As a result, your beliefs and expectations may change so that the situation or event becomes less of a threat.

Date:

From each completed questionnaire, state your total score. Then identify up to three significant stressors for each.

Type A Behaviour (from page 93)	**Work attitude** (from page 99)	**Life events** (from page 103)	**Work stress** (from page 106)
Total score:	Total score:	Total score:	Total score:

My **three** most significant stressors from each questionnaire:

1	1	1	1
2	2	2	2
3	3	3	3

Figure 8.2 Summary of my stressors.

1
2
3

Date:

Figure 8.3 My three key stressors.

You have now completed the groundwork necessary to devise your stress management plan. Now comes the important part of managing stress – working out an effective plan to deal with your stressors. To do this you need to *build up your knowledge of techniques* to use in your plan. Keep your three key stressors in mind as you read and work through the following chapters on dealing with stress. Some coping techniques prepare you to handle general pressures and demands, while others are more appropriate for specific stressors. In Chapter 15 you will be guided further on how to work out and implement your SMP.

Part three of this book deals with a range of stress management techniques that affect the stress response. These include:

- *changing demands*
- *learning to relax*
- *reviewing lifestyle*
- *modifying Type A Behaviour*
- *increasing love and support*
- *enhancing self-esteem*
- *encouraging laughter and humour.*

The above are just a few of the many different therapies and techniques that may be effective in stress management planning.

In addition, we have selected a number of techniques and reviewed these in Appendix II. These techniques have been selected because they are known to affect the activity of the stress response, and are, therefore, an important source of information and a resource in stress management planning:

- *cognitive behavioural therapy*
- *neuro linguistic programming*
- *hypnotherapy*
- *music therapy*
- *aromatherapy*
- *orthomolecular vitamin redox regimes.*

Stress management planning does not have to include exclusively recognized or formalized therapies, techniques or products to deal with stress. Making adjustments in day-to-day activities may help to alleviate stress for an individual. Whatever helps or works for you goes, as long as it is legal and does not offend others.

9

Improving coping ability

In this chapter you will learn:
- *about assessing your coping ability*
- *skills for building up coping*
- *about achieving the right balance between coping and demands.*

To deal with stress effectively, you must adjust your stress balance to keep it in and around the normal zone. This means not going too far and too often into the distress zone and making it easier to enter and remain in the eustress zone when the need arises. Getting the right balance is achieved by adjusting the weight in the pans. Clearly there are two ways in which this can be done: either by altering demands or by improving coping ability (Figure 9.1, pages 117–8).

Having read Parts one and two of *Manage Your Stress for a Happier Life*, you now know one of the most important ways of dealing with stress – being *aware* of it. You will know what is happening in your body when your stress response is activated. You should now be able to recognize physical and mental signs of over-activation of the stress response. You should have some insight into how this can affect your health and performance. Furthermore, you should be able to identify personal sources of stress.

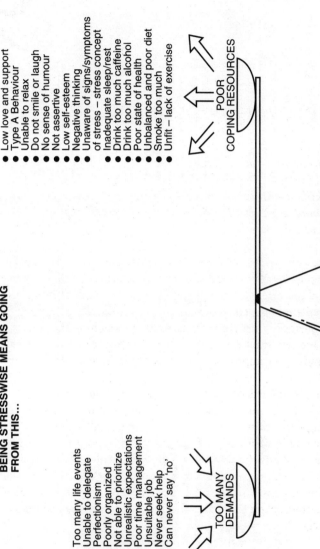

BEING STRESSWISE MEANS GOING FROM THIS...

- Too many life events
- Unable to delegate
- Perfectionism
- Poorly organized
- Not able to prioritize
- Unrealistic expectations
- Poor time management
- Unsuitable job
- Never seek help
- Can never say 'no'

TOO MANY DEMANDS

- Low love and support
- Type A Behaviour
- Unable to relax
- Do not smile or laugh
- No sense of humour
- Not assertive
- Low self-esteem
- Negative thinking
- Unaware of signs/symptoms of stress – stress concept
- Inadequate sleep/rest
- Drink too much caffeine
- Drink too much alcohol
- Poor state of health
- Unbalanced and poor diet
- Smoke too much
- Unfit – lack of exercise

POOR COPING RESOURCES

Figure 9.1 Factors altering demand and ability to cope.

9. Improving coping ability   117

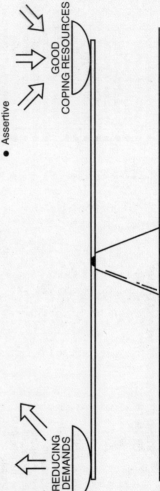

... TO THIS

- Keep count of life events
- Can say 'no'
- Organizes
- Prioritizes
- Realistic expectations
- Avoids perfectionism
- Able to delegate
- Seeks help when necessary
- Good time management
- Avoids uncertainty
- Suitable job

REDUCING DEMANDS

- Awareness of stress concepts
- Can recognize signs and symptoms of stress
- Able to relax – practise relaxation techniques
- High love and support
- Good state of health
- High/secure self-esteem
- Low Type A Behaviour
- Healthy balanced diet
- Low/moderate alcohol and caffeine consumption
- Reduce/stop smoking
- Exercise regularly – fit
- Smile and laugh
- Good sense of humour
- Positive thinker
- Assertive

GOOD COPING RESOURCES

Figure 9.1 (contd) Factors altering demand and ability to cope.

You are now in a position to think about your own stress and learn how you can manage stress more effectively. There are many different techniques for doing this. Those described here are the ones we found most useful and effective in teaching our groups and individuals. There is inevitably much overlap between the contents of each and, because of this, there is some repetition of information and advice. However, we feel this will serve to emphasize the importance of the issues we describe, their relationships with one another and the holistic approach we advocate for dealing with stress.

Before you start, you can assess your current coping ability by completing the following questionnaire.

COPING ABILITY

Tick either Yes or No to each question.	Yes	No
1 Do you have supportive family/friends?	❏	❏
2 Do you have a hobby?	❏	❏
3 Do you belong to a social or activity group?	❏	❏
4 Do you practise an active relaxation technique (yoga, meditation, imagery, autogenic training, etc.) on a daily basis?	❏	❏
5 Do you exercise for at least 20 minutes three times a week?	❏	❏
6 Do you do something 'just for yourself' each week that you really enjoy?	❏	❏
7 Do you have somewhere you can go in order to be alone?	❏	❏
8 Have you attended a stress management, relaxation, time management or assertiveness training course?	❏	❏
9 Do you show Type B Behaviour?	❏	❏
10 Do you smoke?	❏	❏

(Contd)

11 Do you drink alcohol to relax?   ❏   ❏

12 Do you take sleeping pills?   ❏   ❏

13 Do you take work home?   ❏   ❏

14 Do you drink more than eight cups of caffeinated   ❏   ❏
    drinks (coffee, tea, coke, chocolate) each day?

15 Do you show Type A Behaviour?   ❏   ❏

For scoring and evaluation turn to page 229.

For scoring and evaluation turn to page 229.

YOUR COPING ABILITY

Items 1 to 9 can help you deal with pressures and demands when practised regularly. If you answered yes to items 10 to 15 then you may be using these strategies to deal with pressures and demands but in the long run they could be a threat to your health.

List your most commonly practised coping strategies:

GOOD COPING STRATEGIES (Items 1 to 9)	POOR COPING STRATEGIES (Items 10 to 15)
----------------------------------	----------------------------------
----------------------------------	----------------------------------
----------------------------------	----------------------------------
----------------------------------	----------------------------------
----------------------------------	----------------------------------
----------------------------------	----------------------------------

---

Use these lists to focus your attention on developing appropriate and effective coping strategies as you read through the next five chapters.

Insight

Change unhealthy coping strategies for good healthy coping strategies.

Getting the right balance

When the balance tips into the distress zone (perceived demands outweigh perceived ability to cope), adjustments can be made to reduce demands (Figure 9.2) or to build up coping resources so that the balance swings back into the normal zone.

We will inevitably encounter situations in which demands outweigh our ability to cope. No matter how much our coping resources are increased, demands have the potential of being one step ahead. For example, it is certain that we will be confronted by novel situations as part of daily living. Furthermore, from time to time our ability to cope can be reduced by changes in our general state of health, allowing demands to get the better of us when we are not feeling so good.

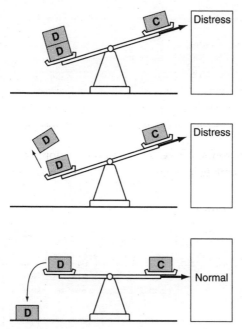

Figure 9.2 Getting the right balance: reducing demands.

Normally we would not have given these demands a second thought. Nevertheless, building up your coping resources so you have plenty of reserve will enable you to deal with extra and taxing demands without tipping your balance too far into the distress zone (Figure 9.3).

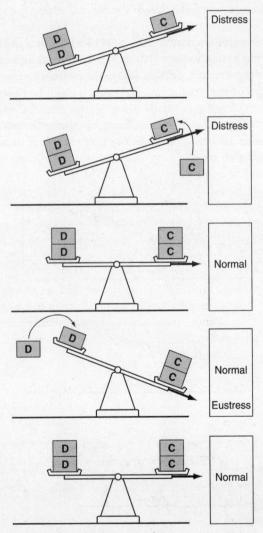

Figure 9.3 Getting the right balance: building up coping resources.

Adjusting your balance in this way is achieved by preparing yourself
to keep one step ahead of 'reasonable' demands by learning skills to
build up your coping resources. For most of the time this will keep
you in the normal zone but with a season ticket to enter the eustress
zone. However, additional and excessive demands will inevitably
arise and tax our ability to cope. So increasing your coping reserves
will help lessen the blow and keep you away from the depths of the
distress zone – avoiding the bad and ugly!

Ironically, under some circumstances, thinking we have too much
ability to cope can also cause distress. This can occur in two
ways. First, when the perceived demands may be too few and
consequently do not balance our perceived ability to cope. We
can then feel under-used; we feel we have the ability to do more
and our skills and expertise are not being utilized. Clearly, it is
not appropriate to say to someone in this situation, 'Go away and
reduce your coping reserves to match your level of demand'. The
right balance is achieved by increasing demands (Figure 9.4).

Second, if we have unrealistic views of our abilities to handle
demands, we may perceive that we can cope with more and more
when in fact we cannot. To avoid tipping the balance into the
distress zone, we must be realistic about our expectations thus
reviewing our ability to cope.

Adjusting the balance is a continuous operation of altering demands
and coping resources. You are the only person who can adjust your
stress balance.

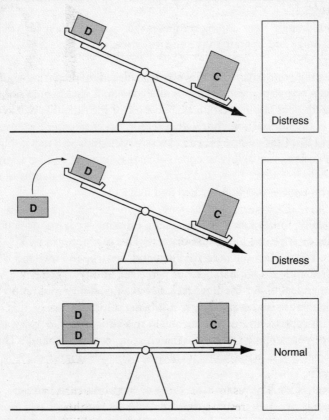

Figure 9.4 Getting the right balance: increasing demands.

10

Altering demands

In this chapter you will learn:
- *about the need to review demands*
- *ways of reducing demands*
- *ways of increasing demands.*

Reducing demands

KEEP COUNT OF LIFE EVENTS

Insight

Too many changes in a relatively short period can tax your ability to adapt, resulting in distress and ill health.

To avoid this problem, always keep an eye on your number of life change events. Use the life events list on page 103 as a checklist and keep a tally of your score.

Try to prevent too many of these events occurring in a short time. So, for example, if you have just changed jobs, moved house to an area miles from your family and friends and taken on a mortgage, it would be wise to postpone other plans or projects until you have settled. If you are nearing retirement, consider making a gradual rather than a sudden change from full-time work to full retirement.

Traumatic life events, such as divorce, serious illness or death of a loved one, are likely to reduce your coping reserves. This will make you more vulnerable to the dangers of distress. At such times it would be wise to consider the number of demands you are dealing with and to build up your coping resources through love and support (see Chapter 14).

The life events list is by no means exhaustive. You should identify events in your life which require an adjustment in order for you to handle them. These can be pleasant as well as unpleasant events. Give each a score according to your judgement of how they compare with the events and scores shown on the life events scale.

For each and every one of us, there is a one in ten chance (ten per cent risk) that we will suffer a serious illness during the next two years. But your life events score during the previous year may increase your risk of ill health during the following two years (see the table below). So scoring 150 to 299 points will increase your chance to about one in two (50 per cent risk). This may be a result of excessive cortisol release since many life events require attention over a relatively long period. Under these circumstances, cortisol can reduce our ability to fight infection and makes us more susceptible to disease.

Score	Risk of illness during next two years
300 or more	80%
150–299	50%
100–149	30%
less than 100	no change in risk

Note that the life events scale is based on studies of many thousands of people, so this scale is not very accurate in predicting the illness vulnerability of individuals. This is because each of us will perceive the events differently and the ability to cope with them will vary considerably from individual to individual. Nonetheless, it is wise to consider the effects on our health and performance of accumulating stressors.

LEARN TO SAY 'NO'

Some people find it very difficult to say 'no' to requests from friends and work colleagues, even though they feel unable to cope with more work. They often feel it is a sign of lack of cooperation or an admission that they cannot handle their work. They feel that refusing to help may prejudice their promotion prospects or affect their relationship with others.

More work here does not just mean work connected with our jobs but also requests to join another fund-raising event, coach the local football team, service the car, decorate the house and so on. As the saying goes, 'If you want something doing, always ask a busy person because they are usually the ones who are unable to say 'no'!'

If you feel you cannot take on more work then be honest, clear and assertive in your reply. Point out how much you are currently doing and what is waiting to be done, or that there are circumstances in your domestic life making it difficult for you to work extra hours.

It is important that you say 'no' in the right way. Julie, a secretary, told us about her main source of stress at work. 'My boss always gives me a pile of work at around 4.00 p.m. and expects it to be completed before I finish work at 5.00 p.m. Sometimes I'm still typing at 6.00 p.m.' We asked why she had never said anything, 'I'm afraid he will think I'm not being cooperative and I might lose my job.'

We pointed out the consequences of her distress and suggested she asked her boss to prioritize the work in the following way. 'I realize that this work is important; however, I finish work at 5.00 p.m. and when you give me work at this time of the day I'm usually here until 6.00 p.m. I have an important appointment tonight so I would appreciate it if you would kindly sort out those items that are urgent and I'll make sure they are done before I leave. I will come in early tomorrow morning and deal with the rest.'

So what happened when Julie tried this way of saying, 'No, I'm not prepared to tackle all those demands'? Mr Smith did just as she asked. In fact, he designated only two letters as urgent. Julie left work at 5.00 p.m. and tells us that she has only worked later than that on two occasions since. Julie's response was assertive. She stated her case clearly and honestly, was firm and polite and suggested what might be done to help resolve the situation. Being assertive will help you say 'no' in the right way (see page 202).

Whatever the situation or circumstance, one thing is certain: if you take on more than you feel able to handle, then you are likely to feel pressured, harassed and rushed, and your performance will suffer. Jobs will take longer to do and may not be done well. So saying 'no' and seeking clarification of priorities, planning ahead and being realistic about what you can achieve makes sense in the long run.

ORGANIZE YOUR LIFE, PRIORITIZE AND BE REALISTIC ABOUT WHAT YOU CAN ACHIEVE

Some people find it helpful to plan ahead: from day to day, week to week, month to month and year to year. Others have the philosophy of 'live for today' which reminds us not to be too obsessed with rigidly organizing the future. However, even carefree people must plan ahead in some way or another. This should include setting priorities and being realistic about what can be achieved.

SETTING REALISTIC GOALS

Many unnecessary demands can result from setting unrealistic goals which are difficult to attain. This is particularly true for Type As. Being realistic about what you can achieve will reduce demands. This will mean being honest about your abilities. Winning promotion to a job you have always wanted but find you cannot handle is one of the major sources of distress.

Insight

To set your priorities and realistic goals, take a piece of paper and write your objectives and goals in life.

Use the following headings:

| Self | Family | Friends | Work |

Write down everything, even those things you feel are impossible to achieve. Here are a few suggestions to help you:

Self
- ▶ *Stop smoking*
- ▶ *Need more exercise*
- ▶ *Need to lose weight*
- ▶ *Need time to relax*
- ▶ *What would I do if I had more time?*
- ▶ *What do I enjoy doing?*
- ▶ *Learn a new skill or subject*
- ▶ *Would like to travel more*

Family and friends
- ▶ *Spend more time with them*
- ▶ *Visit relatives more often*
- ▶ *Like a different house or new car*
- ▶ *Help children more with school work/projects*
- ▶ *Take trips out together*
- ▶ *Need to make new friends*

Work
- ▶ *Type of work*
- ▶ *Commuting distance*
- ▶ *Shift work and working away from home*
- ▶ *Work abroad*
- ▶ *Ambitions*
- ▶ *Start my own business*

Now, for each item identify the importance you attach to it. Grade the importance by using five stars for top priority and one star for the least. Now go through the list again and mark those items that you feel you can realistically achieve with an 'R' or highlighter pen. Delete those items which you feel are too difficult to attain or are unattainable. Now sit back and review your list. You may need to decide on a timescale for some items – what your goals are for the next month, year and so on. Construct a short-term and long-term plan. You will probably realize that many of your goals are achievable simply through minor changes in your lifestyle, perhaps devoting a little more time to one area rather than another.

By undertaking this exercise you are planning your life, prioritizing your activities and being realistic about what you might achieve. In this way you will have more chance of fulfilling your expectations. When expectations are achieved, self-esteem is high and this will enable you to deal more effectively with stress. Frequent failure to achieve unrealistic goals severely damages self-esteem and opens the door to aggression or depression.

Clearly, circumstances change, so you will need to update your lifeplan regularly, maybe weekly or monthly. You may find it an interesting exercise to construct your lifeplan at this stage of the book and again when you have finished reading it.

ORGANIZING AND PRIORITIZING

Insight

Planning and prioritizing your work can help you reduce and avoid distress.

Much anxiety can build up if the tasks that need to be completed seem never-ending. We start to wonder how and when to fit in other essential activities. Look at your work schedule, prioritize and plan the order of completion, considering deadlines and importance. It is not much use spending a lot of time and effort on minor tasks, and perhaps getting tired and irritated, when more important and urgent jobs need to be completed, and done well. Try to concentrate on one task at a time, particularly if this is a major and important one.

One man described to us how he dealt with his office letters, memos, reports and so on. 'I start reading a document on the top of the pile of papers on my desk. I get halfway through and my mind wanders to a letter I caught a glimpse of halfway down the pile. I can't resist leaving the document I'm reading to pull out the letter. I start reading the letter, think 'Yes I must do this, that or the other' and then push it to one side. I go back to the first document and, having lost my train of thought, I start at the beginning. Soon I'm off into the pile again. As a result I don't seem to get things done very quickly and end up thinking and worrying about several things at the same time!'

Our advice to this man was to prioritize: Sort quickly through your papers and put them in order of importance. Make three piles and colour-code them: very urgent (green – go), urgent (amber – get ready) and not urgent (red – stop). Work through each pile in turn, dealing with the very urgent before proceeding to the urgent and so on. Of course, priorities can change so the order should not be considered fixed.

Wading through a sea of papers is one of today's worst office stressors. You can check your efficiency and your need to prioritize by ticking the corner of a document each time you read or look at it. You may be surprised at the number of ticks some documents accumulate.

Insight
Keeping a diary and appointment book is a very effective way of organizing yourself.

Write as much information as is appropriate about appointments, deadlines and reminders as they arise, for both work and home life. You will need a large enough diary to provide the space for notes and suggestions and drawing up plans for the day and week but this does not mean buying an additional briefcase to hold your 'mega-diary'! In this way you will have less need to make notes on scraps of paper which may get lost. Everything is in one place and time is not wasted wading through piles of notes. Give a high priority to personal and domestic problems since failure to deal with these will inevitably affect your work.

A well-maintained diary will help to reduce the worry and anxiety of wondering whether you will remember all your appointments. Make time every day to work with your diary. Use self-adhesive coloured dots or highlighter pens to prioritize tasks. Keep to the same colour for a specific activity: purple for deadlines, blue for meetings, yellow for telephone calls, for instance.

Insight

Avoid creating unnecessary deadlines and cluttering up your calendar with appointments.

Use the heart paperclip from *Stresswise* (see page 240) to mark the day of the week in your diary. This will serve as a reminder that ignoring the effects of excessive demands can be costly to both your health and work performance.

An important factor in planning and setting priorities is being realistic about what can be achieved. If you are asked to give a time for completion of a task, do not put yourself under unnecessary pressure by saying next week (just to make yourself look efficient) when you know you may not meet that deadline.

AVOID PERFECTIONISM

Perfectionists in particular need to be realistic. Type As are bugged by perfectionism. Always striving obsessively to achieve perfection is usually counter-productive. Many perfectionists believe that if perfection is not achieved, disaster is bound to result. It must be realized that the 'perfect and best' result can only be achieved once in a lifetime. Striving to better your best performance each time leads to unnecessary demands, pressures, distress and feelings of failure if it is not achieved.

Insight

Settle for your best effort and be content with what you have done.

You probably will have produced a good and satisfactory job without ending up distressed.

Perfectionism as described here should not be confused with working conscientiously and diligently to achieve your best performance and good results, particularly where it is essential for tasks to be done correctly. So getting rid of perfectionism does not mean attending less to your work and making mistakes or producing poor performance. We describe perfectionists as those people who are obsessive about producing a 100 per cent absolutely correct piece of work in everything they do.

Why do perfectionists strive for perfection? We asked a self-confessed perfectionist to tell us about the advantages of perfectionism. She said, 'It sometimes produces an excellent piece of work which pleases me very much.' 'Are there any disadvantages?' we asked. She thought for a while and replied, 'Yes I suppose there are. I often worry about not doing a good job. This means I usually stick to techniques I know well so I hardly ever experiment with new ideas. I am self-critical, set myself high standards, get very upset if things are not turning out the way I want them to. Sometimes I spend such an incredible amount of time trying to produce a perfect result that I become agitated. Usually I end up settling for what I had achieved in the first place. In the meantime, I waste a lot of time and feel annoyed with myself.'

Another key factor in planning and prioritizing is managing time. Learning the skills to manage your time effectively can reduce demands and increase coping ability, thus helping tip your stress balance into the eustress zone. Some aspects of time management are dealt with in the section on modifying and reducing Type A Behaviour (see page 191).

DELEGATE

Another way of reducing demands at home and work is to delegate. If you are in a position to delegate at work then you have undoubtedly demonstrated that you are good at your job and you are probably managing, supervising and directing others. There can be a tendency for you to believe (particularly if you are Type A) that jobs will get done better and quicker if you do them all yourself, but this is often not the case. You can become overloaded with tasks which could be delegated to someone else.

When you delegate, make sure you choose the person best suited to the job and who has the time to devote to it. Give clear instructions and information about what you expect and reassure the person of your confidence in them and that you will be available should they need any advice or assistance.

There are many positive benefits to delegating. Giving responsibility to another person makes them feel part of what is going on, that you have confidence and trust in them, and it provides them with the experience they will need for their career advancement. Their self-esteem is boosted and they will probably perform well with their stress balance in the eustress zone.

Individuals can often face a mountain of demands if they have multiple roles. Looking after the home or family, planning or preparing meals, shopping, cleaning etc. This job is frequently combined with employment outside the home. Clearly, reducing demands by delegating domestic duties can help avoid distress.

Seek help when the going gets tough
Seeking help and support from others in the tasks you perform can be mutually beneficial in reducing workload and demands. Rather than struggle, ask for help. Struggling on your own can be very distressful and will certainly make a task more difficult to complete.

Insight
It is better to admit you need help with a demand and then go on to satisfactorily complete it, than to struggle on your own to end up producing a poor piece of work, or even failing to complete it.

FIND A JOB WHICH SUITS YOUR PERSONALITY AND ABILITIES

If you are looking for a job, you should seek one which you feel suits your personality, skills and ability. If you are already in a stressful job, then review the demands placed upon you and your abilities to handle them. Consider your work expectations and be realistic about your ability to achieve them.

Learn to work effectively
Many aspects of your work may be decided by your employer or organization, leaving you with little control over what you do. In situations where this is distressful, stand back and ask yourself whether the demands and pressures are real and reasonable or whether your perceived lack of control is a result of your unrealistic expectations.

Clearly, the physical conditions of your work environment are important, not least from a safety point of view: bad lighting, insufficient heating, poor ventilation, noise, overcrowding, lack of privacy and uncomfortable office furniture are frequent sources of dissatisfaction, frustration and distress. Many employers appreciate that the right physical environment will encourage productivity and creativity, so you should not be hesitant about approaching your employer if you feel these things are causing you distress. There are some changes you can probably make for yourself such as brightening your immediate work area with coloured posters, postcards, photographs, cartoons and plants.

There is much you can do to organize your work. Take short breaks from routine tasks even if it means simply closing your eyes for a few minutes and relaxing. Practise a relaxation technique (such as those described in Chapter 11) at your desk or bench. Arrange your office or surroundings so you have to get up and walk to the filing cabinet or to answer the telephone. When you talk on the telephone, concentrate on the task in hand and do not polyphase (do more than one thing at a time). Be assertive, say 'no' when you feel overloaded with work. Seek immediate clarification about what is required when you are asked to do a job. At this stage you should point out any difficulties or problems you foresee and ask for help if necessary. It is always more difficult to do this after the event, though you can always go back and ask again. In the meantime, you may have worried unnecessarily over difficulties and problems.

If you have a lot to do, arrange your jobs in order of priority. It is usually most productive, effective and satisfying to complete one job at a time before moving on to the next.

Do not rush; spend some time thinking about how to tackle problems and plan your course of action. Routine jobs are often best tackled using a strict timetable such as opening mail first thing in the morning. Do not clutter your diary with appointments or make appointments when you know you may not be able or will be pushed to keep them. Leave some time for yourself during the day for relaxation and never miss your lunch and tea breaks. Use them effectively: get out of the work environment, go for a walk or relax and read a novel. Learn to manage your time effectively.

Most people work with others, so you should pay particular attention to giving and receiving support and building self-esteem with respect to your work. Learn the art of good communication and assertiveness. Develop the art of listening – you will not only learn more by listening rather than talking but you will form better relationships – people like to talk and tell you about themselves. Control your voice in discussions; do not become threatening or emotional. You will get your views over better by using clearly stated points in an assertive manner. Do not underestimate the value of good humour.

AVOID UNCERTAINTY

> **Insight**
> Uncertainty is the cause of much distress.

Worrying about 'what might happen if...' may be unnecessary. Find out the facts about things before you get anxious and panic. When you have collected as much information as you can, it might then be obvious that your initial fears and worries were ill-founded and you will have avoided unnecessary distress. On the other hand, if your worries were warranted you will be prepared and can plan all the possible alternatives and seek help if necessary. This will make you feel less uncertain. Coping with demands and pressures is easier if you know exactly what you are dealing with.

Increasing demands

There are a number of situations where an individual may feel that there are too few demands in their life: too little stimulation and not enough challenges. They feel they have the capacity to handle more. They feel under-used, bored and frustrated. Self-esteem suffers, motivation declines and eventually performance becomes poor in all they do.

One situation where this may arise is retirement. This can involve a sudden change from active and busy full-time work to a less demanding life with few deadlines to keep. As a retired person, you can experience an overnight change from being an important part of an organization and making a valuable contribution to society, to a position where your usefulness within society seems diminished. It is not possible to reduce your perceived coping ability to match your lower perceived demands, so you should take on new demands. Maybe take up a hobby, join an evening class and learn something that you always wanted to do but never had the time for while working. Plan and do the things you did not have the time for, such as taking a long trip abroad. Keep up and renew friendships, become involved in community projects, local clubs and voluntary organizations. Plan your day as if it were a working day; build in time for domestic duties, shopping, walking, hobbies, and so on. But beware – do not increase demands to the point where your stress balance tips into the distress zone.

Another situation where too few demands lead to distress is where an employee feels their abilities and skills are not adequately used. The remedy is to ask the employer for more work. On the other hand, it may be that someone in this position is in the wrong job. Finding the right job to suit your aptitude and abilities is not an easy task. Where there is a significant mismatch, distress inevitably results. Correcting this situation may mean requesting the organization to reappraise the job role with a view to moving you to a different job or it may mean leaving the job and seeking one which is more suitable.

We can find ourselves in a position of having too few demands if we lose our job, face a change in family situation when children leave home or our partner dies. When we get back on our feet it may be necessary to increase demands in a similar way to the retirement situation described above.

10 THINGS TO REMEMBER FROM CHAPTERS 8, 9 AND 10

1 *Practising a stress management plan may enable you to avoid potential stressors and to deal more effectively with those you encounter.*

2 *Learning skills to reduce or increase demands and building up coping resources will prevent unnecessary and harmful stress.*

3 *Keep your life events under review, as too many changes in a relatively short period can tax your ability to adapt, resulting in distress and ill health.*

4 *Write a list of your objectives and goals in life; set your priorities and make your goals realistic.*

5 *Planning and prioritizing your work can help you reduce and avoid distress.*

6 *Keeping a diary and appointment book is a very effective way of organizing yourself.*

7 *Avoid creating unnecessary deadlines and cluttering up your diary and calendar with appointments.*

8 *Avoid perfectionism; settle for your best effort and be content with what you have done.*

9 *It is better to admit you need help with a demand and then go on to satisfactorily complete it, than to struggle on your own to end up producing a poor piece of work, or even failing to complete it.*

10 *Uncertainty is the cause of much distress; find out as much as you can and work through scenarios so that you are prepared.*

11

Learning to relax

In this chapter you will learn:
- *several techniques for relaxation*
- *training procedures for relaxation*
- *what the benefits are of learning to relax.*

Recharge your batteries

A period of relaxation is a time to recharge your batteries. It is
a period of minimal sympathetic nervous system activity which
allows the parasympathetic nervous system to increase its influence
on body function. When you are relaxed, your noradrenaline,
adrenaline and cortisol levels are lowered and your body activity
is opposite to that experienced during the activation of the stress
response. Heart rate and breathing decrease and the body feels
warm due to dilation of the blood vessels. Sweating decreases,
saliva secretion increases, muscle tension decreases, and the mind
feels settled. However, your body is always ready to respond to
danger within a split second even from a deep state of relaxation.

DEVELOP RELAXING DAILY ACTIVITIES

There are a number of specific procedures that bring about a state
of relaxation, for example yoga, meditation, progressive and deep
muscular relaxation, autogenics, self-hypnosis and biofeedback.
Many of these procedures must be learned and practised regularly.

Insight

Practising a relaxation technique should become part of your life – just as brushing your teeth twice a day, you should actively relax every day, and not just when you are feeling or expect to feel stressed.

Learning these techniques takes time and you should not expect too much too soon. Furthermore, it can take a while before the benefits are experienced but the results are worth waiting for. Later we describe the techniques we use and take you through the procedures so you can learn to achieve a state of relaxation.

There are also a number of activities that can be built into your daily routine to make you feel relaxed and revitalized. Taking a hot bubble bath, floating in a swimming pool, taking a steam bath, sauna or jacuzzi can bring about a state of relaxation. So too can going for a pleasant walk, taking a weekend break away from home, listening to your favourite music (Baroque music appears to be particularly effective), reading your favourite books, a night out at the theatre, an evening meal at your favourite restaurant.

Massage is a particularly effective way of relaxing the muscles which in turn leads to a calm mind. Also taking up a hobby, a leisure activity, joining a club, tinkering with the car, tackling a DIY project or developing new interests can all be relaxing as long as they are looked on as relaxation activities. But beware, some of these activities can be stressful if tackled in the wrong way.

A well-planned holiday of at least a week's duration is a good way to recharge your batteries. However, take heed, even a holiday can be packed full of distress. There might be airport delays, language and currency problems and there could be plenty of rain instead of 'guaranteed' sun. Stomach trouble can strike, you get sunburnt, and your partner forgot to pack your favourite beachwear. What is intended to be a relaxing holiday can turn into a distressful nightmare! Preparation and planning can help avoid many of these problems and minimize distress.

QUIETING REFLEX – QR

Step one	Close your eyes. Pinpoint in your mind what is annoying or stressing you.
Step two	Say to yourself, 'Alert mind, calm body. I'm not going to let this get to me.'
Step three	Smile to yourself. You can practise smiling to yourself without showing a smile on your face. In this way, your smile will not be obvious to others around you.
Step four	Breathe in to the count of three while imagining that the air comes in through holes in your feet. Feel the sensation of warmth and heaviness flowing throughout your body, starting at your feet and ending at your head.
Step five	Breathe out to the count of three. Visualize your breath passing through your body from your head and out through the holes in your feet. Feel the warmth and heaviness flow through your body. Let your muscles relax, let the jaw, tongue and shoulders go limp.

Now open your eyes and resume your normal activity.

Relaxation should not be regarded as something done only outside work. Taking your regular coffee and lunch breaks is important; these are times for you to recharge your batteries. Try to get away from your office or work surroundings. Go for a short walk or read a favourite book. If you feel stressed during the day, sit back for a few minutes and practise a quick relaxation technique. Try the quieting reflex (QR). It takes only a few seconds and with practice achieves a body state opposite to activation of the alarm reaction.

With practice over several months, QR becomes automatic. It provides a pause for you to decide whether or not to stay stressed, tense and annoyed or to shift into a less irritated and more relaxed state.

Are you breathing correctly?

This may seem an obvious question: 'How,' people ask, 'can an everyday automatic activity like breathing be carried out incorrectly?' This is more of a problem than you may imagine. Incorrect breathing can cause much discomfort, ill health and a feeling of distress. A part of our stress response is to change breathing patterns. During physical exertion, breathing rate and depth increase, because we need to take in more oxygen to eliminate the vast amount of carbon dioxide produced by muscle activity. The chest moves outwards and upwards to allow more air into the lungs. When we breathe at rest, it is movements of the diaphragm that exchange the air in our lungs. As the diaphragm moves up and down, the abdomen moves in and out but the chest remains almost stationary.

In emotional stress, activation of the stress response leads to rapid breathing. The upper part of the chest is mainly used for this type of breathing. With no physical outlet for our stress response, such breathing (called hyperventilation) flushes too much carbon dioxide out of the lungs, making the blood and tissues more alkaline.

In some situations breathing can become rapid and very shallow from the chest. Insufficient air is taken in and out of the lungs to flush out the accumulating carbon dioxide so it builds up in the blood, making it more acidic. These patterns of breathing which make the blood too acid or too alkaline can result in abnormal body functions.

Our breathing pattern can reveal our emotions. Anxious people breathe rapidly and talk as they breathe in (inhale). On the other hand, depressed people sigh frequently and talk as they breathe out (exhale). If people remain in state of high sympathetic arousal and anxiety for a long period, their breathing pattern can alter at rest and during moderate activity. Over time their breathing shifts more from diaphragmatic movement to chest movement.

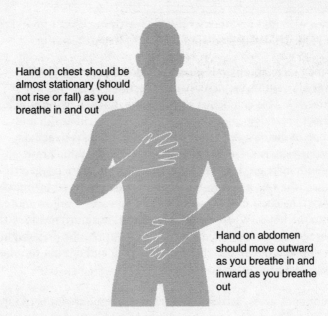

Hand on chest should be almost stationary (should not rise or fall) as you breathe in and out

Hand on abdomen should move outward as you breathe in and inward as you breathe out

Figure 11.1 Are you breathing correctly?

So, are you breathing correctly? Try this simple test. Lie on your back in a comfortable position, support you head on a pillow and relax. Place one hand on your abdomen and the other on your chest (Figure 11.1). As you inhale and exhale note the movement of your abdomen and chest. If you are breathing correctly, the hand on your abdomen should rise as you breathe. So, if the hand on your abdomen is stationary then you are breathing incorrectly.

PROCEDURE FOR CORRECTING YOUR BREATHING AND USING DEEP BREATHING FOR RELAXATION

Lie on the floor on your back. Support your head on a pillow. Bend your knees, keeping your feet flat on the floor. Place one hand on your chest and one hand on your abdomen. Breathe slowly through your nose. Keep your mouth closed. Take slow gentle deep breaths. As you *inhale* push your abdomen out against your hand – feel your abdomen expand and your hand rise. Hold for two seconds* and then *exhale* slowly through your nose. Feel your stomach deflate and your hand fall. Repeat four times.**

When you have mastered this exercise, follow the same procedure in the sitting and standing position. Eventually, you can do the exercise without positioning your hands on your chest and abdomen. Concentrating on your abdominal movements in this way will slowly help to correct faulty breathing patterns. The procedure can be used as a relaxation technique in its own right, when you feel tense and anxious. It is a useful quick method that can be applied almost anywhere – sitting at your desk, in a stationary car, on a train or bus.

Correct breathing and the deep breathing techniques are used in most other forms of relaxation such as the two we describe later. So before attempting these, practise the breathing exercise.

Use biofeedback

Skin resistance meters are relatively inexpensive devices suitable for self-help purposes. More sophisticated and expensive equipment is needed to obtain biofeedback from other body activities such as brain wave activity. However, a very simple and inexpensive device for self-help is the biodot. We use these simple devices in our *Stresswise* programme.

Biodots are small self-adhesive temperature-sensitive discs that can be stuck to the skin, usually on the inner surface of the wrist or at the base of the thumb and forefinger. They indicate changes

* Sufferers from respiratory complaints including asthma and bronchitis may find breath-holding uncomfortable or difficult. These sufferers should avoid long breath-holding in this exercise and others described later.
** For everyone: Stop the breathing exercise if you feel light-headed at any time during the procedure and resume your usual pattern of breathing until you feel able to continue.

in skin temperature caused by differences in the amount of blood flowing through the skin. More blood-flow – skin is warmer; less blood-flow – skin is cooler. When a person is tense and stressed, blood vessels constrict, reducing skin blood-flow, thus lowering the temperature of the skin. The biodot will appear yellow, amber or black. When a person is calm and relaxed blood vessels dilate, increasing skin blood-flow, and this raises the temperature of the skin. The Biodot will appear green, turquoise, blue or violet.

Biodots are available from *Stresswise* (see page 240) and their use will assist you in learning to relax.

Biofeedback is the use of instruments and devices to enable a person to monitor body responses triggered during the stress response such as heart rate, blood pressure, muscle tenseness, skin temperature, sweating and brain electrical activity. The technique allows the user to see for themselves their level of stress response activation and state of relaxation. Biofeedback is a useful tool for relaxation training, as it will indicate to the user whether or not a state of relaxation has been achieved.

One of the most commonly used methods involves measuring the amount of sweat on the skin. During the stress response sweating increases; in the relaxation response it decreases. The amount of sweat on the skin is detected by two small metal plates (electrodes), each strapped to a finger. A small, safe electrical current is passed across the electrodes. When the skin is moist, due to the presence of sweat, the current passes easily over the skin. When the skin is drier, the passage of the current is impeded because the skin resistance is higher. So this technique measures the skin resistance and is known as the galvanic skin response or GSR. In fact, GSR techniques form the basis of lie detector apparatus. Usually when a person tells a lie, their emotions trigger the stress response, leading to sweating.

For biofeedback information, the skin resistance is converted into a sound. Increased stress and tension lead to a high-pitched sound, relaxation results in a lowering of the sound.

Skin resistance meters are relatively inexpensive devices suitable for self-help purposes. More sophisticated and expensive equipment is needed to obtain biofeedback from other body activities such as brain wave activity.

Progressive and deep muscular relaxation

In this technique, each of the main groups of muscles is tensed then relaxed (progressive muscle relaxation – PMR). At each stage the mind is concentrated first on the feelings of tension and then on relaxation. With practice, you can learn to be aware of muscle tenseness so you can easily and automatically convert tension into relaxation. For example, many drivers find their shoulders hunched and hands gripping the steering wheel so tightly that the knuckles turn white. Through PMR, you will recognize this tension and automatically relax the muscles, thus reducing head, neck, shoulder and back pains and stiffness.

When the body muscles are relaxed, the mind relaxes and this reduces sympathetic nerve activity, leading to a decrease in heart rate and blood pressure. However, the technique is not recommended for sufferers with high blood pressure (hypertension). This is because the tensing of the muscles causes elevation of the blood pressure which then decreases when the muscles are relaxed. So if you suffer with hypertension it is not wise to increase your blood pressure further by tensing the muscles during PMR. Instead we advise you to practise deep muscular relaxation (DMR). This technique is similar to PMR but the muscles are not deliberately tensed prior to relaxing (page 150).

You will need to find a suitable place to practise these techniques: somewhere quiet and warm, where you will not be disturbed. It is advisable not to try them for up to two hours after eating a heavy meal, and use a firm, upright chair rather than an armchair, which can encourage drowsiness. It is helpful to get someone to read the procedure to you so you can concentrate on the movements and technique. Alternatively, ask someone with a soft, relaxing voice to record the instructions (we have deliberately written them almost

as a commentary) and play the recording or CD back to yourself.
A pre-recorded audio-cassette of these procedures is available from
Stresswise (see page 240).

PROCEDURE FOR PROGRESSIVE MUSCULAR
RELAXATION (PMR)

> **Warning: Do not over-tense or over-stretch your muscles.**
> Stop if you feel uncomfortable or experience any pain. Sufferers
> with high blood pressure are advised to practise deep muscular
> relaxation instead of using PMR.

Allow 15 minutes.

- ▶ *Sit comfortably, well back in the chair, so your back is
  supported and both feet rest flat on the floor, a little way
  apart. Place a biodot on your hand. Rest your arms in your
  lap. Keep your head straight with your chin parallel to the
  floor. Your breathing should be abdominal and relaxed –
  gentle, slow and unforced.*
- ▶ *Close your eyes and direct your attention to each part of your
  body in turn. As you tense each set of muscles, concentrate on
  the tenseness and tightness (hold the position for five seconds
  or so) and then as you relax the muscles, concentrate on the
  sensation of relaxation. Notice how the tenseness disappears
  and the muscles feel at ease, warm and heavy (stay in this state
  for about ten seconds).*
- ▶ *Shrug your shoulders towards your ears – pull them up as far
  as you can – feel the tenseness in your shoulders and neck.
  Hold for five seconds. Now relax; feel the muscles relax.
  Relax for ten seconds.*
- ▶ *Now pull your shoulders down towards the floor. Concentrate
  on the tenseness. Hold it. Now relax.*

[Always hold the tenseness for about five seconds and the
relaxation for about ten seconds.]

- ▶ *Bend your right arm and make your bicep muscle stand out
  as much as you can; tense the muscle, hold it... now lower the*

*arm and relax. Turn the palm of your right hand upwards.
Clench your right fist as firmly as you can. Concentrate on
the tenseness and relax, unfolding your fist. Now stretch your
fingers out as far as they will go, feel your fingers stiffen and
the thumb pushing away from the fingers. Hold it, feel the
tenseness and relax; feel the fingers curl gently inwards.*

▶ *Bend your left arm and make your bicep muscle stand out;
tense the muscle, feel the tenseness; lower the arm and relax.
Turn the palm of your left hand upwards. Clench your left fist
as firmly as you can and concentrate on the tenseness. Hold
it... now unfold your fist and relax. Stretch your fingers as
far as they will go. Feel the fingers stiffen, the thumb pushing
away from the fingers. Hold it... now relax and notice the
fingers curl gently inwards.*

▶ *Concentrate on your legs. Straighten your right leg and push
your foot away from you; feel the tenseness of the muscles
on the front of your thigh. Point your toes as far away as
you can, now bend your foot back at the ankle. Feel the calf
muscle tense in your right leg. Hold it... and relax. Tighten the
muscles in your right foot. Curl your toes and when your foot
feels as tense as you can make it... relax.*

▶ *Straighten your left leg and push your foot away from you;
feel the tightness of the muscles at the front of your thigh.
Point your toes as far away as you can, now bend your foot
back at the ankle. Feel the calf muscle tense in your left leg.
Hold it... and relax. Tighten the muscles in your left foot.
Curl your toes and when your foot feels as tense as you can
make it... relax.*

▶ *Now lift yourself up by tensing your buttock muscles. Lift
higher and higher – hold it... now let the muscles relax.*

▶ *Contract your abdominal wall muscles – make your waist as
small as you can. Feel the tenseness. Hold it... and relax.*

▶ *Now turn your attention to your head. Move your head gently
forward until you feel the muscles in your neck and back
tighten. Hold it and then return your head back to the centre
and relax. Tilt your head to the right, feel the tenseness in your
muscles and then return your head to the centre and relax.
Now tilt your head to the left, feel the tenseness and return
your head to the centre and relax.*

▶ *Now clench your teeth tightly; feel the pressure and tenseness of your jaw muscles. Allow your jaw to sag slightly, feel the muscle tenseness ease. Let your mouth drop open and feel the tenseness ease further... and relax. Now close your mouth and push your tongue against the roof of your mouth; feel the tenseness and pressure... now relax the tongue behind the lower teeth. Relax.*

▶ *Smile broadly; feel the change in muscle tenseness; hold it... and relax. Screw up your eyes, tighter and tighter. Hold it... and relax them back into the sockets. Now pull your eyebrows down, now raise them as high as you can, hold it... and relax.*

▶ *Concentrate on your breathing: feel your abdominal muscles move slowly out and up as you breathe in and then down and inwards as you breathe out. Your breathing should be slow, gentle and shallow.*

▶ *Now quieten your mind. Allow your thoughts to drift through your head, without trying to pursue them. As easily as thoughts come into your mind they leave, and as easily as they leave more thoughts effortlessly come in. Recall happy memories. Picture a walk along the seashore: the waves, warm water lapping around your feet as they sink in the sand. Sun glistening on the water. Deep blue cloudless sky. The cries of the gulls.*

▶ *Sit quietly for five minutes and enjoy the state of relaxation you have created throughout your body. Your body should feel warm and heavy – totally relaxed.*

▶ *After five minutes open your eyes slowly. Look at your biodot.*

▶ *Before you stand up, gently stretch your body and take two or three deep breaths.*

PROCEDURE FOR DEEP MUSCULAR RELAXATION (DMR)

Allow 15 minutes.

▶ *Sit comfortably, well back in the chair, so your back is supported and both feet rest flat on the floor a little way apart. Place a biodot on your hand. Rest your arms in your lap. Keep your* head straight with your chin parallel to the floor. Your breathing should be abdominal and relaxed – gentle, slow and unforced.

▶ Close your eyes. Direct your attention to each part of your body in turn. Each time, relax the muscles and concentrate on the sensation of relaxation. Notice how tenseness disappears and muscles feel at ease, warm and heavy (stay in this state for about ten seconds).

▶ Concentrate first on your left leg. Focus your attention on each part of your leg in turn, starting at your toes and working towards your hip. As you relax each set of muscles, feel the tension drain away and notice the sensation of limpness, heaviness and warmth. Relax your toes... concentrate for about five seconds on the feeling of relaxation (do this between relaxing each part). Now relax the instep... heel... and ankle. Now relax your leg muscles... feel them become limp, heavy and warm. Now relax your knee... thigh... and your hip. Concentrate on the relaxation of your left leg... heavy, limp and warm.

▶ Now focus your attention on your right leg. Concentrate on each part of your leg in turn, starting at your toes and working towards your hip. As you relax each set of muscles, feel the tension drain away and notice the sensation of limpness, heaviness and warmth. Relax your toes... concentrate for about five seconds on the feeling of relaxation... now relax the instep... heel... and ankle. Now relax your leg muscles... feel them become limp, heavy and warm... now relax your knee... thigh and your hip. Concentrate on the relaxation of your right leg... heavy, limp and warm.

▶ Now concentrate on your left arm. Focus your attention on each part of your arm in turn, starting with the fingers and working towards your shoulder. Relax your fingers and thumb... feel them curl inwards... relax your palm... now your wrist... forearm... elbow... upper arm... and lastly your shoulder. Concentrate on the limp, heavy and warm sensation.

▶ Now concentrate on your right arm. Focus your attention on each part of your arm in turn, starting at your fingers and working towards your shoulder. Relax your fingers and thumb... feel them curl inwards... relax your palm... now *your wrist... forearm... elbow... upper arm... and lastly your shoulder. Concentrate on the limp, heavy and warm sensation.*

▶ *Now concentrate on your stomach muscles. Let them relax... limp, heavy and warm.*

▶ *Now concentrate on the base of your spine. Slowly work your way up the spine towards the neck, relaxing each part of the spine and associated back muscles as you progress towards the neck. Feel the muscles relax, becoming limp and heavy as your back sinks into the chair...*

▶ *Now relax your shoulders again... feel them drop towards the floor, limp, heavy and warm...*

▶ *Relax your neck muscles but keep your head straight, your chin parallel to the floor. Your head should now be balanced on your spine.*

▶ *Now focus your attention on your head. Relax your jaw, let it drop and feel your mouth slightly open... relax your tongue and feel it drop behind your lower teeth... relax the muscles around your eyes... feel them become limp, heavy and warm... relax your forehead... and scalp. Your head should feel totally relaxed, heavy and warm.*

▶ *Concentrate on your breathing: feel your abdominal muscles move slowly out and up as you breathe in and then down and inward as you breathe out. Your breathing should be slow and gentle.*

▶ *Now quieten your mind. Allow your thoughts to drift through your head, without trying to pursue them. As easily as thoughts come into your mind they leave, and as easily as they leave more thoughts effortlessly come in. Recall happy memories. Picture a walk along the seashore: the waves, warm water lapping around your feet as they sink in the sand. Sun glistening on the water. Deep blue cloudless sky. The cries of the gulls.*

▶ *Sit quietly for five minutes and enjoy the state of relaxation you have created throughout your body. Your body should feel warm and heavy – totally relaxed.*

▶ *After five minutes open your eyes slowly. Look at your biodot.*

Meditation

Whereas PMR and DMR concentrate on muscle relaxation, meditation concentrates on relaxing the mind. The technique is straightforward. The mind is focused for 20 minutes on a word or sound, known as a focal device. This is repeated over and over again in the mind. As the technique is performed, thoughts will pass in and out of the mind. When the mind wanders it can be brought back to the focal device. With practice, the mind will wander less often as the repetition of the word engages the left side of the brain in a meaningless task. This side of the brain deals more with logical and analytical thinking and normally dominates our consciousness (Figure 11.2). When the word is repeated over and over again the left brain is occupied in the monotonous task of attending to the repetitious information. As this happens, the activity of the right side of the brain takes over. This side of the brain is involved with intuition, imagination and creativity. Suppressing the analytic activity of the left brain and allowing intuitive dominance of the right brain results in a reduction in stress response activation and an increase in tranquillity; a feeling of serenity.

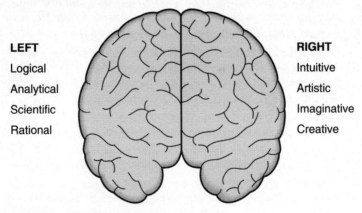

LEFT
Logical
Analytical
Scientific
Rational

RIGHT
Intuitive
Artistic
Imaginative
Creative

Figure 11.2 The left and right hemispheres of the brain.

During meditation, the body's oxygen requirement drops, the heart and breathing slow, blood pressure decreases. In fact, a general state of relaxation is achieved. Recordings of brainwave activity show more alpha rhythms which are characteristic of a state of relaxation.

There are a variety of meditation methods, but the basic technique is a very effective and beneficial relaxation tool which can be used by everyone. The meditation procedure we describe below uses a word as the focal device. Like PMR and DMR, meditation can be undertaken anywhere reasonably quiet, warm and free of possible distractions. **Note:** It may not be suitable for those suffering from epilepsy and some psychiatric disorders.

PROCEDURE FOR MEDITATION

Allow 20 minutes.

- ▶ *Find a quiet, warm place where you will not be disturbed. Sit in a comfortable, upright position. Place a biodot on your hand. Make a note of the time. Breathing should be slow, gentle and abdominal. Close your eyes then repeat aloud the word 'om' or 'one'. Do this several times then repeat the word more quietly and then quieter still, until you are not moving your lips but merely thinking the word over and over in your mind. Do not concentrate on keeping the word in the forefront of your mind – it should not be like counting sheep. You will find that your mind begins to wander. Thoughts will come into your mind: 'I've got to buy some postage stamps on the way home', 'I must book the car in for a service'.*
- ▶ *Let thoughts wander into your mind and then let them leave by thinking the sound over and over again. (The sound of the word is purely a means of helping you clear your mind.) Continue in this manner for 20 minutes, then stop and sit quietly for a minute or so.*
- ▶ *Gradually and slowly open your eyes. Look at your biodot. Look for the signs of relaxation such as warm hands and feet, and salivation.*
- ▶ *End your relaxation by gently stretching your arms and legs and taking two or three slow deep breaths.*

Do not use an alarm to tell you when the 20 minutes is up – open your eyes slowly and look at a clock when you feel that 20 minutes has passed. With practice, you will find it easy to judge 20 minutes. The time will seem to pass very quickly. Sometimes you will find it hard to believe you have sat and relaxed for 20 minutes. After practising meditation regularly, twice a day for about two to three months, you may experience periods of deep mental relaxation. If, however, this does not happen, do not become concerned. It is the process of relaxing that is important. Continue with the procedure.

Try to meditate regularly each morning and evening at a time when your home or office is reasonably quiet. Take precautions so you will not be disturbed. While you are learning the technique, you may find it helpful to use earplugs (available from chemists). Unplug the telephone and ensure the room temperature is comfortable. Avoid eating for about two hours beforehand. Late evening meditation may affect your sleep since meditation usually increases alertness.

We recommend you practise PMR, DMR and meditation in the sitting position without supporting the head. If you are lying down, with head supported in a relaxed state, it is easy to fall asleep. The aim of practising a relaxation technique is to achieve a state of physical and mental calmness different from sleep.

Insight

Relaxation techniques must be learned and you should not expect instant success.

Eventually, you should be able to take a short meditation or muscular relaxation anytime and anywhere.

The benefits of relaxation

The reduction in sympathetic nervous system activity brought about by relaxation techniques has the benefit of allowing the body to rest and recharge its batteries. Your coping abilities usually increase, making it likely that you will experience eustress rather than distress. However, there are a number of other benefits. Some doctors now use relaxation methods, particularly PMR, DMR and meditation, to treat patients with high blood pressure and high blood cholesterol, sometimes without the use of medication. In the same way that blood pressure and cholesterol levels rise as sympathetic arousal increases, so levels drop when sympathetic activity declines. Patients practising relaxation for one month or more have shown a decrease in blood cholesterol and other blood fats.

It has been reported that regular meditators make fewer visits to their doctors than non-meditators, and that a variety of physical ailments can be alleviated through meditation. While teaching relaxation techniques, we have seen some remarkable changes in our students. A 38-year-old woman with Raynaud's disease (painful cold fingers due to constriction of the digital arteries) reported that the condition disappeared two weeks after she learned to meditate. Three years later, she has not experienced the symptoms again. We have taught many people with sleep problems to meditate. In most cases their problems have disappeared within a week or two of starting meditation. A woman on tranquillizers managed to reduce her dose under the supervision of her doctor after we taught her to meditate. It must be said that these problems might have disappeared anyway or that it was not the meditation itself but the care and attention given to these people that did the trick. Maybe so, we cannot prove otherwise, but there is enough evidence to support the belief that the biological consequences of meditation can bring about such changes. A number of studies and surveys also support this view.

Other benefits of relaxation, and particularly of meditation, are increased mental alertness, improved concentration, creativity and memory, leading to better performance and enhanced or improved relationships. Regular practice can lead to improved wellbeing and a different, more rational attitude and view of life.

12

Lifestyle review

In this chapter you will learn:
- *the importance of reviewing lifestyle for managing stress*
- *a biological explanation of lifestyle stress effects*
- *about managing lifestyle more effectively.*

There are a number of ways in which you can alter your lifestyle to build up your resistance to stress. If you are healthy and fit you will feel good about yourself: your self-esteem will be high, and your irritability, anger and hostility levels low. The following lifestyle review looks at:

- ▶ *diet*
- ▶ *caffeine consumption*
- ▶ *alcohol consumption*
- ▶ *smoking habits*
- ▶ *fitness and exercise*
- ▶ *body weight*
- ▶ *sleep and rest.*

It is not a comprehensive guide to health and fitness, but deals with some aspects which we feel are particularly relevant to the stress response and its activation and which we use regularly in our workshops.

Diet

We have all been inundated with advice on what to eat and what not to eat, so much so that many people find it confusing and stressful. We hear, 'Eat this, don't eat that, eat more of this and eat less of that'. One minute we are told, 'Eat this,' the next 'Don't.'

> **Insight**
> One thing is certain – when we are stressed, we are more likely to show erratic eating habits. We are more likely to snack on foods with high fat and sugar content (comfort food) but with low nutrients and health benefits.

We suggest that you try to eat foods that help combat an activated stress response by selecting foods that help make us feel calmer. For example, foods high in tryptophan, such as red meat, poultry, fish, eggs, nuts and seeds, will help to increase serotonin levels in the brain which affect the stress response through our emotions, making us feel calmer.

FAT

Despite the massive amount of research into how our diet affects our health and what a healthy diet is, there is still much that is not understood. For example, the link between dietary fat intake and heart disease is far from clear. But the message we are given makes it sound so simple and clear-cut. 'Large amounts of fat in our diet increase blood cholesterol. High blood cholesterol is associated with heart disease.' The latter point is known to be true, but is high blood cholesterol related so conclusively, as we are led to believe, to what we eat? The relationship between diet and blood cholesterol is controversial and extremely complex and the arguments for and against this issue are outside the scope of this book.

So what should we do? It is a question of being sensible about our diet. Eating an excess of anything will cause problems and a little bit of what you fancy will probably do you no harm. To become obsessive about what you eat can cause much distress and feelings of guilt. This could do more harm than the so-called unhealthy diet itself. Of course there are those, such as angina sufferers and heart attack victims, who may need to regulate their diet but for most of us strict rules may not be appropriate. However, everyone can benefit by taking the stress out of eating.

One of the main aims of the fight and flight reaction is to provide a quick and plentiful supply of energy for muscle activity by mobilizing fats and glucose stores. The level of blood fats, including cholesterol, and the level of blood glucose increases. During the alarm reaction, the levels of cholesterol and triglyceride (another type of fat) rise far more than they can from dietary sources. In fact, only about ten per cent of our cholesterol comes from the diet; the rest is made by the body. We described earlier, page 78, how levels of blood cholesterol rise during periods of stress. We used the example of tax accountants meeting deadlines to complete their clients' tax returns. Try to remember this point when you feel pressured because if you are stressed you will have higher levels of cholesterol circulating in your blood than normal.

Remember also that increased blood cholesterol and fat levels are associated with coronary heart disease and increased susceptibility to blood clot formation. For angina sufferers and heart attack victims, one high-fat meal can lead to red cell sludging which can block the fine coronary blood vessels. The result could be a heart attack which may be fatal.

It is therefore wise to reduce your intake of fat, particularly saturated fat, so when your blood fat and cholesterol levels rise during stressful periods, there is less chance of them reaching potentially harmful peaks.

Insight

Eating high-fat meals while you are under pressure and feeling stressed is therefore not to be recommended.

FIBRE

Another way of reducing blood fat is to eat more fibre. It works like this: fats stick to the fibre, which is not absorbed by the body, so the amount of fat absorbed is also reduced. Be careful not to eat too much fibre (the recommended daily intake is 30 grams) because certain vitamins and minerals can also attach to fibre, so less of these will be absorbed into the body.

VITAMINS

It is also advisable to make sure you have enough Vitamin B complex (comprising several different B vitamins), Vitamin E and Vitamin C in your diet, particularly when you feel pressured and stressed. These vitamins are required for a number of vital body processes. Vitamin C is required for fighting infections and wound healing, and Vitamin B complex for good mental activity and many of the body's chemical processes. They are also needed to make the hormones used during the stress response, and there is some evidence suggesting that inadequate Vitamin C levels may encourage the accumulation of cholesterol in arteries. Foods rich in Vitamin C are blackcurrants, rosehips, citrus fruits, leafy green vegetables such as Brussels sprouts and cabbage. Vitamins of the B complex are found in a variety of foods; rich sources are wholegrain cereals, yeast and meat.

Vitamin E is necessary to keep the membranes of our cells healthy and it may play a beneficial role in the ageing process. Rich sources of Vitamin E are vegetable oils, wheatgerm, sunflower seeds, hazelnuts, brown rice and wholegrain cereals.

A well-balanced diet should provide an adequate amount of Vitamin C and B complex; however, to ensure you are not lacking these two vitamins when under stress, it is advisable to take supplements.

Supplements of Vitamin E can also be taken. This should be with a meal since the presence of polyunsaturated fat is necessary for the absorption of Vitamin E. It is advisable to use the natural d-alpha-tocopherol rather than the synthetic dl-alpha-tocopherol (the synthetic form contains only about one-tenth of the natural form, so it is less biologically beneficial for us). Read the labels on the containers carefully.

Vitamins C and E and some minerals, such as selenium, have antioxidant properties. Antioxidants render harmless the toxic chemicals, called free radicals, produced normally by our body. Free radicals can damage the cells of the body and have been linked to a number of disease processes.

Insight

A number of vitamins and minerals, including Vitamins B, C and E, are required for the synthesis of the stress hormones, therefore our antioxidant levels can become depleted during periods of stress. This will expose our cells to potential damage from free radicals, so taking dietary supplements of antioxidants can help counteract the depletion of antioxidants during stress.

EATING A WELL-BALANCED DIET

Your mineral and trace element intake should also be adequate. Although a well-balanced diet should contain essential nutrients in the correct proportions, look particularly at your intake of calcium (good food sources are dairy produce and spinach), magnesium (nuts, cereal grains and fish), iron (red meat and offal, green leafy vegetables and wholegrain cereals), zinc (bran, meat and dairy produce), manganese (wholegrain cereals, nuts and avocado pear), selenium (meat, dairy produce, wholegrain cereals) and chromium (wholegrain cereals, brewer's yeast and cheese). All these minerals are involved in the stress response and deficiencies caused by their depletion during periods of stress can lead to poor body functioning and ill health.

This is not to say that you should increase your food intake when under stress. Rather, by eating a balanced diet in the first place, you ensure that your body is prepared to deal with increased pressure when the need arises. Similarly, protein levels can decrease during periods of stress; an action of cortisol is to mobilize body proteins for energy. So attention should be given to a balanced protein intake during periods of prolonged stress. This is because when we feel distress we often do not feel like food, at the very time we should be taking extra care about eating properly.

It is not advisable to take megadoses of vitamin or mineral supplements except under medical supervision. Subjected to excessive doses, the body can become saturated with the vitamin or mineral and this may hinder or prevent vital body functions. Taking supplements according to Recommended Daily Allowances will do no harm (RDAs are usually shown on the label of the container). Refer to Food Standard Agency website, page 243.

Increased sweating during the stress response can lead to dehydration. Drinking one or two pints of water each day will help prevent this and stop the blood from thickening too much. Thick blood clots more easily.

As well as taking the above precautions, it makes sense to eat a balanced diet; that is, a diet which has both the right number of calories to provide sufficient energy and the right proportions of all essential nutrients. Such a diet comprises about 10–15 per cent protein, 30–35 per cent fat (made up of half saturated and half unsaturated, that is polyunsaturated and mono-unsaturated), 50–60 per cent carbohydrate and adequate vitamins, minerals and water.

For the average person this may mean:

▶ *cutting down on fat intake (particularly saturated fats – these are mainly animal fats)*
▶ *increasing the amount of complex carbohydrate eaten to increase fibre intake (wholegrain cereals, wholemeal, bran, pulses, nuts and seeds) and*
▶ *eating more fruit and vegetables, preferably fresh or frozen, not tinned.*

Eating sensibly is not just a question of eating the right amounts of food but also adopting a sensible eating pattern. It is very easy to miss meals when under pressure. Breakfast can become one cup of coffee and lunch a quick sandwich as you work. On the other hand, life can become one continuous meal when under stress.

Let your body tell you when to eat. Keeping to the traditional 'three meals a day' rule is not always necessary. It is often better to eat smaller, more frequent meals spaced throughout the day instead of eating one or two very large meals. In this way the digestive system does not work 'overtime'.

Breakfast is considered by nutritionists to be the most important meal of the day – it gets us off to a good start. Skipping breakfast leads to mid-morning tiredness, irritability, depression, confusion and an inability to concentrate. Ideally, breakfast should contain unrefined carbohydrates, protein and some fat, for example porridge, low-fat sausages, low-fat yogurt, or fresh fruit. This provides a steady level of blood sugar throughout the morning. Lunch should be a top-up meal and the evening meal the lightest of the day. It is better to eat your evening meal early because the digestive processes may cause sleeplessness. Eating a light evening meal will give your digestive system a rest overnight.

The types of food we eat can also affect our mental activities. What we eat as well as when we eat can affect our memory and ability to concentrate.

Insight

Meals excessively high in carbohydrates and low in protein make it less easy for people, particularly those over 40 years old, to concentrate and deal with mental tasks.

Our diet can help us to combat stress effectively, so:
▶ *eat a well-balanced diet*
▶ *watch your fat intake*
▶ *check your fibre intake*
▶ *make sure your mineral, Vitamin C and B complex intake is adequate*
▶ *consume two litres of fluid each day, mostly water*
▶ *eat breakfast.*

Caffeine

Caffeine, taken in reasonable amounts, has many health benefits. However, excessive consumption is potentially harmful. Since caffeine stimulates the release of the catecholamine stress hormones, the mix of stressful demands and increased caffeine consumption can elevate our stress levels well into the distress zone.

Caffeine is found mainly in coffee, tea, cocoa, drinking chocolate, chocolates and cola drinks.

Excessive caffeine consumption (about 1,000 milligrams of caffeine each day, or six cups of coffee) is considered harmful. Caffeine stimulates the nervous system and production of catecholamines, particularly noradrenaline. It makes sense not to produce more noradrenaline than you need for the activities you are undertaking. Taking an excessive amount of caffeine causes a state of high arousal with your stress reaction operating at full stretch.

Caffeine content of some common beverages in milligrams

		Amount (mg)/ 190 ml cup
Coffee	brewed (filter)	240
	brewed (percolated)	192
	instant	104
	decaffeinated – instant/brewed	3
Black Tea	brewed	50
Green Tea		10
Colas		5–35
Cocoa		5–145
Chocolate		10

Note: these figures are approximate. Actual quantities of caffeine per cup depends on the brand and strength of drink prepared.

Caffeine, through the effects of noradrenaline, increases alertness and performance, but many people find that too much of it during the late evening can lead to sleep disturbances. High caffeine consumers may be addicted to the stimulating effect and pleasant feeling induced by noradrenaline.

Caffeine increases heart rate. Add this effect to the increased heart rate caused by the catecholamines released during stress response activation and you can end up with problems. Such increases in heart rate lead to increased heart workload and can be a danger for those with coronary heart disease. More seriously, caffeine can stimulate the heart to beat irregularly and this can lead to fatal rhythms.

Caffeine also stimulates the production of acid by the stomach. This can cause heartburn and indigestion, and aggravate ulcers. Since the stomach reduces its activity during the stress response, caffeine taken at this time will stay in the stomach longer and have more time to exert its potentially harmful effect. Other digestive tract problems such as colitis and piles can also be aggravated by caffeine.

Insight

There is evidence suggesting that high caffeine intake can lead to increased blood cholesterol through the action of noradrenaline.

Four cups of caffeinated coffee can increase cholesterol in the blood by five per cent and ten cups by around 12 per cent. Such increases, added to the rise in cholesterol during periods of stress, as well as that obtained from the diet, may elevate blood cholesterol to potentially harmful levels.

So try to avoid consuming over 500 mg of caffeine each day. Switch to decaffeinated coffee and herbal teas and other caffeine-free drinks.

▶ *Reduce caffeine intake.*
▶ *Switch to a decaffeinated drink.*

Alcohol consumption

Most people have experienced the effects of alcohol. One or two drinks can be relaxing; three or four and the party takes off! You soon forget your worries. This is the problem; alcohol helps us to forget our distress, so when under stress, some people turn to alcohol to solve their problems. Usually they drink more and more, only to find that when they have sobered up their problems are still there. Unfortunately many people turn to alcohol for its tranquillizing effect. This is clearly not the answer to dealing with problems.

> **Insight**
> Alcohol does not get rid of problems; they will still be there when we have a clear head.

Excessive alcohol consumption can become a health problem leading to a number of physical and behavioural disorders, but many experts believe low quantities of alcohol may have some benefits. The situation is far from clear.

A unit is calculated by multiplying volume (ml) by alcohol content (%) and dividing by 1,000. Just as an example: one 175 ml glass of 12% wine is about 2.1 units (175 ml × 12%/1,000); a 50 ml glass of sherry or vermouth is around one unit (50 ml × 19%/1,000); a single 25 ml measure of 40% spirits is one unit (25 ml × 40%/1,000); a half pint (300 ml) of 3.5% beer or lager is approximately one unit (300 ml × 3.5%/1,000).

The Department of Health recommends that the current safe limit of alcohol intake for men is up to four units each day and for women up to three units. It is important to note that these are the limits for a single day and that it is potentially harmful to accumulate units for a drinking spree over a couple or so days. Also, an alcohol-free day does not mean that you can safely drink more than the advisory limit on the next day. A very helpful and informative booklet is available from the Department of Health. Go to www.dh.gov.uk and type into the search function

'How much is too much? Drinking and you'. This will take you to a list of publications about alcohol use. Scroll down to 'How much is too much' to download the very helpful 16-page pdf.

Like stress, alcohol affects the heart and blood vessels. Moderate amounts of alcohol could be beneficial, but in excess it is certainly harmful, particularly for heart disease sufferers. Alcohol causes blood vessels to relax, leading to an increase in blood flow – a fact that has led to the view that a 'wee tot of whisky' will improve the circulation. This relaxing action of alcohol on the skin blood vessels will make a person feel warmer. A word of warning here for the elderly, a small drink only at bedtimes makes you feel warm and relaxed and will aid sleep, but make sure you are tucked up in bed before you take your drink. If you do not, the dilation of your skin blood vessels means you will lose body heat quickly and this could lead to hypothermia in inadequately heated rooms.

Excessive amounts of alcohol consumed over a long period can cause abnormally high blood pressure, particularly in those who have a family history of hypertension. For this reason people with hypertension should limit their alcohol consumption. Drinking sprees can give rise to abnormal heart rhythms which can be fatal, particularly in those with diagnosed coronary heart disease. This is thought to be due to an alcohol-induced action of the catecholamines, which we know cause cardiac arrhythmias; another reason for not blowing a fuse when you have been drinking!

Alcohol also affects the blood fat levels. First the good news. It appears that HDL-cholesterol ('good' cholesterol) increases with moderate alcohol consumption. This is clearly beneficial, but now the bad news: excessive alcohol consumption causes an increase in the undesirable blood fat levels.

It is the liver that is involved in the breakdown of alcohol and while it is doing so, it cannot attend very well to blood sugar and fat. So fats from the diet tend to remain in the blood rather than be taken up and dealt with by the liver. This results in high blood fat levels which make the blood more viscous, increasing the risk of clot formation and redcell sludging. Heart disease sufferers should keep their alcohol intake low and seek the advice of their doctor on the subject of alcohol consumption. If you do drink more than is advised, then it is sensible to refrain from drinking alcohol for at least two days, so that your liver can recover.

It must also be remembered that alcohol is highly calorific and can lead to weight problems and poor nutrition. One standard unit contains about eight grams of alcohol, providing 56 calories of energy. This is the equivalent of three teaspoons of refined sugar! If you are overweight then think twice before drinking alcohol. While a small amount of alcohol stimulates the appetite, heavy drinkers may lose interest in food. This often leads to poor nutrition and deficiency of vital vitamins and minerals.

Alcohol can destroy self-esteem, family relationships and careers. It can also interfere with sleep and rest – two of the main allies we have for dealing with stress. Alcohol depresses brain function. This leads to impaired judgement and coordination, thus reducing performance and increasing the likelihood of accidents.

All this adds up to the conclusion that a little of what you fancy (but only a glass or two) may be good for you but too much is certainly not, and stress and heart disease definitely do not mix with alcohol. So keep track of your daily and weekly alcohol consumption and stay within the recommended limits. Try switching to low-alcohol, low-calorie drinks and mineral waters.

> ▶ *Keep alcohol consumption within the recommended limits.*
> ▶ *Avoid drinking sprees.*
> ▶ *Try switching to low-alcohol drinks and mineral water.*

Smoking

It is not the purpose here to enter into the 'whether or not to smoke' debate. There is, however, much medical evidence associating smoking with a number of diseases including lung cancer, heart disease and circulatory problems. Many smoking-related diseases are also cited as being stress related, so it makes sense not to smoke.

However, some people smoke to cope with their demands and pressures. Simply having a cigarette in their hand can lower reactions to potential stressors which would otherwise cause distress. Who is to say which is worse for these people – the harmful effects of smoking or those of stress? We recommend using healthy coping strategies (as we describe in this book), rather than an unhealthy (smoking) coping strategy. Research evidence indicates that smoking, together with potential stressors, can lead to a stress response activation higher than the effects produced by either smoking or stress alone. One reason for this may be that, during the stress response, breathing is more rapid and deeper, thereby allowing more cigarette smoke to enter the lungs than during more relaxed conditions.

Nicotine is the main culprit as far as the stress response is concerned. Again, like caffeine, nicotine stimulates the production of the catecholamines, particularly noradrenaline. This may be a reason why smokers tend to have lower levels of Vitamin C in their body (Vitamin C is used in the production of stress hormones). As we pointed out earlier, lack of Vitamin C may cause the deposition of cholesterol in the arteries and could be part of the reason why smoking is linked to coronary heart disease.

It has been suggested that smokers smoke to maintain high levels of noradrenaline which stimulate the pleasure centres of the brain. Noradrenaline addiction again? Nicotine also stimulates the heart, increasing its rate, and the blood vessels, causing them to constrict. Both these effects can exacerbate heart and circulatory disease problems: coronary heart disease, hypertension and intermittent claudication (cramps in the legs due to poor circulation).

It is not only nicotine that is to blame. Carbon monoxide in cigarette smoke combines with the oxygen-carrying haemoglobin in the red blood cells, reducing the blood's oxygen levels. Both carbon monoxide and nicotine cause the blood to clot more easily.

For some people, there can be some beneficial effects of smoking. Nicotine, through the effects of noradrenaline, increases alertness and good performance, benefits associated with the fight aspect of the alarm reaction. However, smokers are not usually fighting or exercising, so the benefits of nicotine are not used in an appropriate way.

Recently, much evidence has accumulated to suggest that breathing other people's cigarette smoke, known as passive smoking, can be harmful to health. So where possible avoid passive smoking. At times, this may mean asking someone not to smoke and doing this assertively will avoid unnecessary distress that can easily arise in such situations.

▶ *Reduce or stop smoking.*
▶ *Avoid passive smoking.*

Fitness and exercise

The alarm reaction was designed for fighting or running away, in other words, for increased activity. When we exercise, essentially the same alarm response is put into action but without the accompanying emotions. For our ancestors and grandparents, life was far more physical: pulling ploughs and walking miles used up the higher levels of circulating blood fats and catecholamines produced by their stress response. Today, it is up and down escalators and lifts and using the car for the shortest of trips. We live in an age of inactivity. Studies have shown that our schoolchildren are the most unfit they have ever been. One man said to us that the PMR programme was the most exercise he had taken for years! It is also an age of psychological stressors and emotional crises. These trigger our stress response, preparing us for action when in fact little muscular activity takes place. However, because of our generally sedentary lifestyle there is a reluctance and sometimes little opportunity to burn off the action of the catecholamines. Arguing on the telephone switches on the alarm reaction, but we are sitting motionless – apart from maybe pounding the desk. So, the actions preparing us for fight or flight are not used. We put the telephone down and we are left with high levels of circulating blood fats and glucose and blood that will clot more easily. The best way to get rid of these is to exercise. Take a brisk walk at lunchtime or after work. If you are upset at the office and feel signs and symptoms of distress, leave the office for a few minutes and walk up and down the stairs. This way you can avoid or reduce the symptoms of distress and will feel relaxed and ready to work productively. Staying in the office will only keep you in touch with the source of your distress.

Regular moderate exercise of 30 minutes a day changes the body's metabolism and helps maintain a desirable body weight. Recent research suggests that the 30 minutes need not be taken in one session but can be accumulated over the day. Exercise is an essential part of any slimming campaign. Furthermore, regular moderate exercise helps reduce the LDL-cholesterol ('bad' cholesterol) in the blood and increase HDL-cholesterol ('good' cholesterol) which is thought to give protection against heart disease.

Warning: Too much exercise without periods of rest produces too much cortisol which can lead to weight problems.

Regular exercise leads to fitness. Feeling fit will increase your sense of wellbeing. You will feel good about yourself and therefore more able to face the demands and pressures of life. Exercise will also improve the quality of your sleep – another essential part of your coping resources.

Exercise need not be expensive. You do not have to rush out to buy the latest in sports fashion wear, or aids such as exercise bicycles and multigyms. Walking and many other activities such as swimming and cycling are relatively inexpensive.

One important benefit of exercise and fitness activities is the possibility of increasing social contacts and developing new friendships at clubs or on an afternoon walk. Exercise and fitness training should be fun and not a chore or too competitive. You will need to find an exercise that suits you – your abilities, schedule, personality. As a general rule choose an activity that would have been done in the days of your grandfather. For example, take up walking rather than squash, especially if you are unfit.

Do not rush into an exercise regime (Type As take note!), particularly if you are over 35 years old. Have a check-up with your doctor, particularly if you are an angina or heart attack sufferer, before you embark on an exercise programme. Always follow a programme which starts slowly and gradually increases to your prescribed level. Do not push yourself too hard. If you have pains (particularly in your chest) or breathlessness, do not ignore them – stop at once and see your doctor as soon as possible. Better to be safe than sorry – exercise can kill!

Avoid exercising when you are unwell, particularly when suffering from flu and other infectious diseases, because infections can spread more easily to the heart muscle and this may lead to serious problems. Try not to exercise too soon after a meal. You should never exercise to the point where you do not have the breath to hold a conversation. Always keep a check on your heart rate by taking your pulse (Figure 12.1) and stay within the safe limits shown in the following table:

Maximum exercise pulse rate per minute

Age	Unfit person	Fit person
20	140	170
30	130	160
40	120	150
50	110	140
60	110	130
70 and above	90	120

For an individual these rates are only a general guide since there are many factors, such as general state of health, to take into account. You should consult your doctor before embarking on an exercise programme.

How do you decide on your level of fitness? A simple test is to check how fast your pulse returns to normal after you exercise. For fit people this usually occurs within a minute or two. If it takes a long time you are probably unfit.

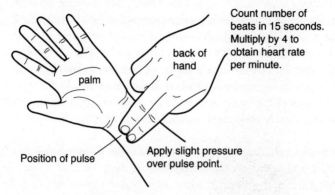

Count number of beats in 15 seconds. Multiply by 4 to obtain heart rate per minute.

back of hand

palm

Position of pulse

Apply slight pressure over pulse point.

Figure 12.1 Measuring your pulse rate.

In the meantime, consider walking to the shops instead of taking the car, walk to work instead of taking the bus, or get off a few stops before your destination and walk the rest of the way. Use the stairs instead of the lift. Ten minutes brisk walk two or three times a day will soon build up your stamina, particularly if you choose an uphill course. Walking is the cheapest, easiest and safest way to exercise and achieve fitness.

> ▶ *Use the stairs, not the lift.*
> ▶ *Walk all or some of the way to work.*
> ▶ *Exercise every day.*
> ▶ *Learn to exercise while you are waiting.*

Body weight

Being overweight (or obese) is unhealthy and can cause much distress. Obesity has been cited as a contributory factor in diabetes, heart and circulatory disease. Obesity can lower self-esteem and cause emotional problems. But how overweight do you have to be to increase your risk of ill health? It seems that the risk grows with an increasing level of obesity. A slight degree of obesity carries a slight risk and being excessively overweight carries a high risk.

A helpful and informative source on body weight matters is Weight Wise at www.bdaweightwise.com.

Body weight depends on a number of factors, so how do you know if you are at your ideal weight, overweight or underweight? Taking height and age is not an accurate method of assessing this. Instead, a measurement called the body mass index (BMI) is used. It is calculated by using the following method or calculated for you on the Weight Wise website at www.bdaweightwise.com/lose/lose_bmi.html.

The ideal BMI for men is around 23 (acceptable range 20.5 to 26) and around 21 for women (acceptable range 19 to 23).

CALCULATING BODY MASS INDEX (BMI)

Step 1   Take your weight in kilograms or convert your weight in pounds to kilograms by multiplying by 0.45.

Step 2   Take your height in metres or convert your height in inches to metres by multiplying by 0.025.

Step 3   Square your height in metres, that is, multiply height in metres by itself (height in metres multiplied by height in metres).

Step 4   Divide weight in kilograms by height in metres squared.

Example – Male

Height 5ft 6in, or 66 inches. Weight 160 pounds.

Step 1   160 pounds × 0.45 = 72 kilograms
Step 2   66 inches × 0.025 = 1.65 metres
Step 3   1.65 × 1.65 = 2.72
Step 4   72 ÷ 2.72 = 26.47. This is the BMI in kg/m².

So for the example above, the man's ideal weight should be 23 × height squared, that is 23 × 2.72 = 62.56 kilograms. To convert kilograms to pounds divide by 0.45. In this case it is 139 pounds so he is about 21 pounds overweight (160 − 139 = 21). A BMI of over 30 carries a real health risk.

Caution must be employed when using BMI to assess levels of obesity, since some individuals may have a high body muscle mass which could raise their BMI to indicate high levels of 'fatness' or obesity, when in fact they are not fat. Their BMI is more a measure of their muscularity rather than of their body fat mass.

So, recognizing this, another measure of 'fatness' has been introduced. Waist to hip ratio measurement looks at body shape and assesses the distribution and amount of body fat. Too much fat around the middle or waist is considered to be unhealthy, particularly as far as the heart and circulation are concerned. Typically, fat around the stomach region produces an apple-shaped appearance, whereas fat around the hips and thighs gives a pear-shaped appearance. The apple shape is considered to be potentially unhealthy. Waist measurement alone can be a predictor of health problems and is described at www.bdaweightwise.com/lose/lose_waist.html along with how to take the measurements.

To calculate your waist to hip ratio: using a tape measure, take two readings in centimetres, first around the narrowest point between the hips and bottom of the ribs, and then around the widest point of the hips. Divide the waist measurement by the hip measurement to give the ratio. So, for example, if the waist measurement is 94 cm and the hip measurement is 105 cm, divide 94 by 105 to give the ratio, which in this case is 0.89.

A ratio of less than 0.85 for a woman and 0.9 for a man is considered healthy. A ratio greater than one is considered to indicate a health risk.

Waist to hip ratio can be calculated for you at
www.stocksurgery.co.uk/waisthipcalc.htm.

There are many causes of weight problems. Overeating and lack of
exercise are obvious causes; hormone imbalances and distress are
less obvious. Often being overweight is not the problem itself but a
result of an individual's emotional problems. Lack of stimulation,
leading to distress, can prompt overeating in an attempt to relieve
boredom. This may take the form of picking at food throughout
the day or bingeing, usually with highly calorific, convenience
foods. The answer to boredom is to find something to occupy the
time and to provide a new challenge, such as taking up a hobby,
joining a club or starting a project at home. Lifestyle should be
reviewed to find out why boredom occurred in the first place.
This should then be tackled.

Low self-esteem is often the cause of compulsive eating and
drinking, resulting in obesity which pushes self-esteem down
further. So improving self-esteem (see Chapter 14) can help avoid
weight problems.

There are many advantages of maintaining your ideal weight. It is
easier to become and stay fit when you have less weight to carry
about. You will feel good about your appearance and be more
comfortable with yourself. So no wonder slimming campaigns,
methods and aids flourish. However, there is probably no other
health issue more controversial than slimming. The only answer
to successful weight loss and maintenance of an ideal body weight
is to balance energy (calorie) input (energy from the food we eat)
with energy output (energy expended during your daily activities).

To lose weight, you need to take in fewer calories than you expend.
This should not be attempted in a drastic way by crash-dieting.
Weight loss should be gradual. Eat fewer calories and expend
more energy a little at a time. Assuming that there are no medical
problems, this method is guaranteed to work and costs very little.
You will need:

- to know how many calories are expended in different activities (below)
- to know the calorie content of different foods (page 178)
- to know the number of calories required for your normal body processes (www.healthstatus.com/dcr)
- to take most of your calories in the form of complex carbohydrates such as wholegrain cereals, wholegrain pasta, potatoes and brown rice
- to plan meals and activities
- willpower to avoid tempting high-calorie foods
- time and patience.

The calorie counting method of weight control

Energy expended (kilocalories) in 30-minute activity

Activity	Kilocalories	Activity	Kilocalories
Sleeping	35	Washing and dressing	100
Walking (casual)	100	Light domestic work	75
Sitting eating	75	Sitting (relaxed)	50
Sitting writing	55	Shopping	100
Golf	100	Tennis	175
Swimming	250	Squash	325
Walking uphill	175	Jogging	150
Gardening	150	Driving	70
Cycling	100	Lying, relaxing	40

First, calculate your approximate energy expenditure by noting the calories used up during your daily activities, then estimate your energy intake by calculating your calorie intake. Make a note of the difference: energy expended minus energy consumed. If you want to lose weight your aim is to expend more than you consume. For every 3,500 kilocalories you expend more than you consume, you will lose one pound of body fat. So if you expend 100 more kilocalories than you eat during one day, it will take nearly a month for you to lose one pound. By expending 500 kilocalories more than you take in each day, you will lose one pound each week.

From the charts you will see that expending an extra 500 kilocalories each day is equivalent to two-and-a-half hours walking or two-and-a-half hours cycling or one hour swimming. It is often easier to reduce the number of calories consumed; one chocolate bar is equivalent in energy to one-and-a-quarter hours of walking. If you are overweight and embark on an exercise programme, you can achieve fitness and weight loss at the same time!

Unless a great deal of trouble is taken weighing everything you eat and timing everything you do, it must be accepted that these calculations are only approximations. But crude though it may be, this technique generates an awareness of the principles behind body weight control and if practised sensibly, will normally lead to weight loss.

Remember, we do not eat simply to ensure that we have enough nutrition to live; it is also one of the pleasures of life.

The calorie counting method of weight control

Energy consumed (kilocalories) per average helping

Food	Kilocalories	Food	Kilocalories
Butter and margarine	100	1 fried egg	140
1 boiled egg	80	Milk, skimmed, in tea or coffee	5
Milk, whole, in tea or coffee	10	All-Bran cereal	90
Yogurt, pot	150	1 digestive biscuit	65
Cornflakes	100	1 jam doughnut	250
1 cream cracker	70	Bread, med. slice	80
Boiled rice	130	Bacon, fried (3 rashers)	340
Chicken (roast)	150	Beef steak, grilled	350

Food	Kilocalories	Food	Kilocalories
Sausage (2 large)	280	Banana	50
Potato, boiled	100	Apple (eating)	30
Jacket potato, incl. skin	80	Grapefruit (fresh 1/2)	20
Chips	300	Orange	40
Roast potatoes	140	Chocolate bar	250
Ice cream	100	Sugar, per teaspoon	30
Beer, per pint	180	Coffee, black	0
Tea, no milk or sugar	0	Fruit juice, unsweetened	70
Cheddar cheese	130	Camembert	100

The above table is a selection of the calorific values of food. More extensive lists can be found in the book *Calories and Carbohydrates* (see page 241) and at the weight-loss resources and calorie-counter websites (see pages 244).

Plan your diet so it is not boring and when you eat out, choose your meals sensibly. Eat little and often so that you do not get hungry or feel tempted to eat a high-calorie snack. Eat grilled rather than fried foods. Eat plenty of fresh fruit and vegetables. Try raw carrot; it is tasty and filling. Cut down on fats, sweets, biscuits and cakes.

▶ *Aim to maintain your ideal body weight.*
▶ *Balance energy consumed with energy expended.*

Sleep and rest

Without doubt, one of the most significant factors in our ability to cope is that we have quality sleep for an adequate period. Sleep and rest are essential for survival, health, fitness and wellbeing. Your brain and body systems can work at a different level of activity, allowing your batteries to recharge ready to face another day of stimulation, threats, challenges and activity.

The quality of sleep appears to be more important than quantity, but too much or too little sleep can lead to irritability and poor mental performance. How long should you sleep? This varies enormously from person to person. Most people sleep seven hours each night while some need nine and others only five. Frequently, worry about losing sleep produces more symptoms of lack of sleep than the sleep loss itself.

If you are experiencing regular sleep disturbance, do not worry that this could be leading to ill health or lack of ability to perform. Even if your sleep patterns are erratic, you get more sleep than you think you do; certainly enough to avoid unhealthy consequences and very poor performance. Your body is geared to make sure you get enough sleep, otherwise you would not survive.

Stress is one of the main causes of sleep disturbance – lying awake at night, trying to get to sleep, worrying about current problems or becoming anxious about future events. When you eventually get to sleep, you wake feeling tired and find the worries and anxieties are still there. People who are depressed usually have little difficulty getting to sleep but they often wake early.

It is also important to get the right pattern of sleep. The kind of sleep called rapid eye movement (REM) sleep, which results in dreaming, is very necessary. Dreaming, even if you cannot remember the dream, is the body's way of sorting out information and problems and ensuring that the body and mind have a complete rest. Alcohol as well as tranquillizers and barbiturates all decrease the amount of REM sleep, so after taking them you may wake up feeling tired or depressed. If you have nightmares, this may be a sign of anxiety or depression. Recurring nightmares are a sign of distress. Meditation can reduce the anxiety associated with nightmares and can help eliminate them altogether.

If you have sleep difficulties then try the following:

▶ *Set up a routine that will condition you to get to sleep. Unplug the television, have a warm milk drink (it contains tryptophan, which promotes sleep), clean your teeth and lastly try reading a short, pleasant story in bed.*
▶ *Avoid taking too many naps during the day or evening.*
▶ *Sit up in bed and meditate for five minutes and then lie down.*
▶ *Before going to bed avoid caffeine, too much alcohol and a heavy meal, particularly foods high in fibre and fats.*
▶ *Make sure you get plenty of exercise during the day.*
▶ *If your mind is racing get up and move around; go to the kitchen and make yourself a warm milk drink. When you have calmed down, return to bed and try to think of a pleasant scene where you feel secure. Try to picture it in your mind's eye and concentrate on it.*
▶ *Ensure that your environmental conditions are conducive to sleep – bedroom not too hot or too cold, light rather than heavy bed clothes, minimal noise level. Switch off electrical appliances at the socket (to avoid mains hum) and use well-lined curtains to reduce light levels.*

Insight

Taking a nap can help alleviate and manage stress.

It has been shown in a number of research studies that napping increases productivity and coping ability. In fact, research suggests that we are designed to have two sleep periods each day; a normal night sleep and a short sleep or nap in the afternoon. Around 12 hours after our deepest sleep during the night, our body temperature decreases and we tend to feel drowsy. For most people, this time coincides with the post-lunch period, around 2.00 p.m. In many countries the afternoon nap or siesta is normal practice as it was in pre-industrial England (eighteenth century). Now it seems that our global, technological, rollercoaster workplace has prevented us from carrying on this tradition – we simply do not have time to nap. Even if we were to find the time, sleeping at work has a stigma. It is not seen in the same way as someone going out for a walk or jog. This is not the case in Japan where desk pillows and napping rooms are provided in the workplace. From our own experience and the comments of others, taking a short afternoon nap does indeed recharge the batteries to make us more alert and productive. Sleep experts recommend a nap of no more than around 15 minutes since more than this is regarded as full-blown sleep which can be counterproductive and affect our ability to sleep well at night. It has also been suggested that having a coffee/tea just before a nap can maximize the benefits of the nap as the alerting effects of the caffeine will kick in around 15 minutes after consumption, coinciding with the time when we wake from napping.

Lack of sleep can lead to body weight problems brought on by the hormones that control hunger and satiety – leptin and ghrelin respectively. Studies have shown that lack of sleep for just a few days can lead to a significant reduction in leptin and rise in ghrelin. This triggers our 'hunger' response to encourage eating, particularly of sugary, starchy and salty foods – clearly not good for our ability to manage stress effectively.

▶ *Get adequate sleep and rest.*
▶ *Set yourself a sleep routine.*

10 THINGS TO REMEMBER FROM CHAPTERS 11 AND 12

1 *Practising a relaxation technique should become part of your everyday life and not restricted to when you are feeling or expect to feel stressed.*

2 *Relaxation techniques must be learned and you should not expect instant success.*

3 *When we are stressed we are more likely to have erratic eating habits and without realizing we snack on 'junk' foods.*

4 *Eating high-fat meals while you are under pressure and feeling stressed is not recommended as your blood fat levels will already be elevated due to your stress response activity.*

5 *Take dietary supplements of antioxidants during periods of stress as the body can become depleted exposing our cells to potential damage from free radicals.*

6 *Meals excessively high in carbohydrates and low in protein make it less easy for people to concentrate and deal with mental tasks.*

7 *There is evidence suggesting that high caffeine intake can lead to increased blood cholesterol through the action of noradrenaline.*

8 *Alcohol does not get rid of problems; they will still be there when we have a clear head.*

9 *Too much exercise without periods of rest produces too much cortisol which can lead to weight problems and weakening of the immune system.*

10 *Adequate sleep is essential for wellbeing and dealing with stress; taking a short nap can be effective in alleviating stress.*

13

Modifying Type A Behaviour

In this chapter you will learn:
- *the importance of Type A Behaviour to stress and its management*
- *what to do to reduce Type A Behaviour for more effective stress management*
- *techniques to practise for modifying Type A Behaviour.*

How to get from A to B

- ▶ *Slow down, do not hurry, why race the clock?*
- ▶ *Tackle one task at a time and enjoy it.*
- ▶ *Learn to occupy your time while waiting.*
- ▶ *Organize your daily activities to avoid queues.*
- ▶ *Accept the mistakes and trivialities of yourself and others.*
- ▶ *Avoid getting angry over things you can do nothing about.*
- ▶ *Avoid creating unnecessary deadlines and cluttering up your calendar with appointments.*
- ▶ *Smile and give love and affection.*
- ▶ *Practise being a good listener.*
- ▶ *Learn to relax; look around and appreciate nature and your environment.*
- ▶ *Play games for fun and not to win.*

Insight
Type As, through their beliefs, attitudes and habits, frequently perceive situations as threatening and challenging when no real threat or challenge exists.

A traffic jam or a slow-moving supermarket queue is clearly not life-threatening, but they can provoke anger which activates the aggressive fight part of the alarm reaction.

How does Type A Behaviour arise?

Studies of the prevalence of Type A Behaviour in identical and fraternal twins have shown that Type A is not inherited, although some of its component behaviours, such as aggression and hostility, may be genetically determined. Other studies have shown that Type A Behaviour is learned. Type A children, particularly boys, tend to have Type A parents. Researchers have shown that one of the ways in which children learn to behave in a Type A manner is by copying their parents.

A child's upbringing can result in Type A Behaviour being manifested from an early age. If parents fail to provide unconditional love (love without pre-conditions) or set never-ending standards and expectations, then the child's self-worth and self-esteem diminishes. At school, the child seizes any opportunity to perform well to boost their low self-esteem. Soon, self-worth and self-esteem become measured by achievements, particularly where it is believed these are admired by parents and others. The struggle to achieve and to secure control over their environment continues into adult life, especially in their attempt to climb the career ladder. In doing so, the individual has learned to behave in a way that can be self-destructive in the long run.

Unlearning Type A Behaviour

So if Type A Behaviour is learned, then it can be *unlearned*. Recent research has shown that Type A Behaviour can be modified and reduced. In one study, the Recurrent Coronary Prevention Project (RCPP), over 1,000 men and women who had already had one heart attack were recruited for a programme designed to modify their Type A Behaviour. The study set out to discover whether Type A Behaviour can be modified and whether such modification alters the risk of having a second heart attack. The recruits were divided into three main groups. Group 1 received the usual advice on what to do following a heart attack; for example, advice on diet, exercise and so on. Group 2 were given the same advice but also underwent a programme of Type A Behaviour modification. Group 3 was a control group; they received no treatment at all.

The Type A Behaviour modification counselling programme ran for one year, and the fate of all the recruits in the study was followed in the succeeding three-and-a-half years. The results showed that Type A Behaviour can be modified and reduced. Further, those in Group 2 who significantly changed their Type A Behaviour reduced, by half, their chance of suffering a second heart attack (both fatal and non-fatal) compared to those in either of the other groups.

Another study by the same researchers demonstrated that Type A Behaviour can be modified in healthy individuals, thus indicating that Type As do not have to be ill to have the motivation to change their behaviour.

In both these studies, the Type A Behaviour reduction was accompanied by a decrease in blood cholesterol level, suggesting that the participants were generating less stress for themselves and therefore less catecholamines. Furthermore, those who changed their Type A Behaviour became calmer and more in control of situations. They improved their self-esteem and sense of wellbeing. They became better listeners. They stopped trying to do too many things at once, so they could pay better attention to the particular task in hand. They were more pleasant to be with. Almost without exception, they found that changes in their behaviour not only improved their family and social relationships but actually enhanced their careers!

So the popular image of a Type A individual who is ambitious, highly competitive, aggressive, hard-driving, a high achiever and therefore highly successful is not altogether true. The more relaxed, calmer, unhurried but still ambitious Type B individual proves to be just as successful, or more so, in the long run. The difference is that Type Bs achieve the same goals but without paying the price of ill health. Many companies have seen the benefits of Type A Behaviour modification. They have arranged Type A Behaviour treatment for their employees, recognizing that it improves their work efficiency and productivity as well as maintaining health. This clearly adds up to a substantial financial saving.

Insight

Most of us display some degree of Type A Behaviour so we can all benefit from taking a more Type B approach to life.

Reduction of your Type A Behaviour can be achieved only by examining your beliefs, attitudes and habits; those habits with which you have burdened your life. A chronic sense of time urgency or a tendency to become easily upset and angry over trivia must be discarded or modified. To do this you must substitute new, healthy beliefs for your bad, unhealthy ones. The RCPP objective for treating Type A Behaviour was to change Anger, Irritation, Aggravation and Impatience (AIAI) into Acceptance (of the errors of yourself and of others), Serenity, Affection and Self-esteem enhancement (ASAS).

AIAI TO ASAS

There are a number of ways of tackling this and they all take time to learn and practise; there is no quick way to unlearn or modify what has taken years to learn.

Drilling

As a start, set yourself drills aimed to make you do the opposite to what you normally do. For example, if you get impatient while waiting, then your drill would be to find a queue and practise waiting without getting impatient. Keep a paperback with you to read or a pack of postcards to write to friends or to make notes or plans for a DIY project. You might say avoiding queues is the best answer. Yes, but, being realistic, you cannot get through life these days without queuing at some time or another. If you travel by car you will certainly get caught in traffic jams. In this case, take the opportunity to relax; put the gear in neutral, handbrake on, feet on floor, breathe deeply and slowly, and recall a pleasant memory.

Review your driving habits – do you drive fast? Race the red light? Do a Grand Prix start on green? Overtake and weave in and out of traffic? If so, then set yourself drills such as driving mainly in the slow lane and keeping to one lane.

Make a list of your Type A behaviours using the description of Type A we provided earlier (see page 92) then make a diary of drills appropriate for your treatment. For example:

Monday:	Speak more slowly.
Tuesday:	Tackle one task/thing at a time (instead of polyphasing).
Wednesday:	Keep mainly in the slow traffic lane (instead of weaving from one lane to another to get in the fastest moving lane).
Thursday:	Walk more slowly.
Friday:	Linger at the table (instead of rushing away as soon as you finish eating).
Saturday:	Seek a long queue and practise waiting patiently (instead of getting impatient and irritated).
Sunday:	Leave your watch off and practise being less time urgent (instead of letting time dictate your day).

Each day, concentrate on the specified drill. So for Monday, concentrate on speaking more slowly; for Tuesday do only one task at a time, and so on. Gradually, with regular drilling, you replace your old Type A behaviours with new Type B behaviours. After a while these will become a habit in just the same way as you learned your Type A behaviours which formed your old habits. Without noticing, you will soon be practising Type B behaviours each day of the week and not only on your specified drill day.

Accept that your change from Type A towards Type B will take a long time to achieve. You will find it useful to construct a drill diary for each day of the year. Here is a list of suggested drills to assign randomly to each day of the year. You will need to use each one several times along with your own drills.

DRILLS

- *Walk more slowly.*
- *Speak more slowly.*
- *Say... 'Maybe I'm wrong'.*
- *Leave your watch off.*
- *Listen to music for 15 minutes.*
- *Linger at the table after a meal.*
- *Recall pleasant memories for ten minutes.*
- *Buy a small gift for a friend, partner or family member.*
- *Drive in the slow lane.*
- *Practise listening during conversations.*
- *Notice objects around you: trees, flowers etc.*
- *Practise eradicating hostile grimaces.*
- *Stop fist clenches and knee jiggles.*
- *Verbalize affection for your partner and children.*
- *Observe facial expression (your own and others).*
- *Ask a friend about themselves.*
- *Set aside 30 minutes for yourself.*
- *Eat more slowly.*
- *Practise smiling.*
- *Practise assertiveness.*
- *Seek a long queue and wait patiently.*
- *Read for 30 minutes.*
- *Alter one of your usual habits or ways of doing things.*
- *Substitute understanding for anger.*
- *Soak in a bath for 15 minutes.*
- *Practise anger control.*
- *Visit a museum, art gallery or park.*
- *Contact an old friend – someone with a job or profession different from yours.*
- *Refer to yourself less often in conversations.*

These drills are aimed at alleviating your sense of time urgency and easily aroused anger and hostility.

Cueing

To help you modify your Type A Behaviour use self-adhesive red hearts available from *Stresswise* (see page 240) which remind you to practise your drills. As an alternative to the hearts, you can use small self-adhesive coloured paper dots available from stationers. Place one in the centre of your watch face on the glass as a reminder to rid yourself of your chronic sense of time urgency. Every time you glance at your watch remember your drills.

> ## Insight
> Place a heart on your steering wheel or dashboard as a reminder to rid yourself of Type A driving habits.

Place one on the telephone to act as a cue to tackle one task at a time and not to polyphase while speaking. How about one on your placemat at the dinner table reminding you to eat more slowly and to linger at the table?

A heart paperclip (also available from *Stresswise*) can be used as a cue in your diary. It will remind you to slow down, not to clutter your day with appointments, to avoid creating unnecessary deadlines and to leave some time in the day for yourself.

We deliberately use hearts as cueing devices because of the associations between Type A Behaviour and the heart. Many participants in our stress management programmes find that this association, together with their awareness of the stress response and Type A Behaviour, motivates them more than anything else to modify their behaviour. As a typical example of this, a man related to us his experience while driving at the start of his counselling programme: 'I was sitting in the traffic jam staying in the slow lane but I could feel my noradrenaline start to flow. I looked at the heart on the steering wheel and reminded myself that the way I was feeling could allow noradrenaline to strike at my heart. A traffic jam is not worth dying for so I turned my cassette on, sat back and relaxed. It was interesting watching those ignorant of this fact gambling with their life in more ways than one!'

Monitoring

Regular drilling takes a great deal of willpower. You will find it helpful to ask family and friends to act as monitors. Explain to them what you are doing and ask them to monitor your progress. They can remind you to drill if you lapse into your old Type A ways. The wife of a man on our programme hummed *The A Team* television show theme tune each time her husband lapsed into his Type A ways. Your monitors may also suggest drills for Type A Behaviours you are unaware you possess; Type As are often blind to their own behaviour. Ask your monitors to read the section on Type A Behaviour and invite their comments on the way you behave. Be prepared to listen carefully to your monitor's observations. They can provide you with support and at the same time help themselves to modify their own Type A Behaviour.

Examining your beliefs

ALLEVIATING YOUR SENSE OF TIME URGENCY AND MANAGING YOUR TIME EFFECTIVELY

Question your Type A time urgent belief. Answer true or false to this statement: *'Being time urgent has helped me gain success'*.

If you answer 'true', then think carefully. How successful are you? It may be that any failures are a result of mistakes that could have been avoided if you had been patient and taken time to think and organize, to be creative and innovative. For this reason, some drills are designed to rid you of your haste; for example, eat, talk, walk, drive more slowly and avoid polyphasing.

Ask yourself if frantically switching traffic lanes gets you to work quicker. Carry on driving in your usual manner for the next week and time your journey each day. Then the following week, keep in one lane (where it is possible) and time your journeys. Now take the average journey time for each week. Most drivers find a difference in their journey time of only a few minutes. Now think: is it worth exposing your heart to potentially fatal levels of noradrenaline to save a few minutes each day?

Other drills are aimed to repair damage done by years of time urgency. Type As have little time to recall memories, so some time should be allocated to this activity. Review your life and plan ahead, setting realistic goals.

Years of struggling to do more and more in less time encourages the Type A individual to concentrate on achievements and strategies to gain or maintain control. There is little space in their lives for relaxation or cultural activities. To correct this, stop measuring your life in quantities – number of committees served on, amount of money earned, number of accomplishments, etc. Think instead in terms of quality of life. To help bring this about, your diary should include drills such as reading more (but not technical and financial texts or material associated with your job), visiting museums, art galleries, theatres and observing nature.

When we asked the wife of one of our Type A group participants if she had noticed any change in her husband's behaviour, she said, 'While we were driving in Wales, Peter commented on the beauty of the scenery. He never did this before the course. It may sound a small thing but when you spend all your time rushing about from A to B a change like this is noticeable.' Remember how, in the Introduction, Frank said he now sees more of life and in particular more of the countryside? These are just two examples of taking time for living. Try taking off your watch; you will find that you have all the time in the world.

Insight
Take time to look around to see what pleasurable things can be found.

You will then rid yourself of your obsession with numbers and quantities and instead describe in words the beauty of things surrounding you.

Ask yourself: are you preoccupied with your own attempts to achieve your goals? Workaholics are blind to the fact that they are not giving time to their families. Even major events in the lives of their children go unnoticed. A recent survey of workaholics revealed some disturbing and sad indicators of this exclusive preoccupation with self and ambitions. A small child drew a picture of his family: Mummy, sister and himself – but Daddy was missing. Another child waiting for his father at the airport was reported to have asked several men, 'Are you my daddy?' How often we have heard our reformed Type As sadly express regret at missing so much of their children's development. The missed school sports, parents' evenings, nativity plays and so on. Once gone they cannot be replaced.

Review your activities to make time for the things that are important. Winston Churchill said, 'When a man cannot distinguish a great from a small event, he is of no use.'

Learn how to manage your time effectively. Our lives are dominated by time and for Type As, time is more of a problem than others. We all know there are 24 hours in each day and we like to use our waking hours effectively. Nobody likes wasting time unnecessarily; it is in reality losing part of one's life. But if you become obsessed with time, the resultant distress could be shortening your life and certainly reducing its quality.

Managing your time effectively at work is important if you wish to avoid distress. The section on reducing demands (page 125) suggested a number of ways in which you can do this by planning, prioritizing, setting realistic goals, being assertive, avoiding perfectionism, saying 'no' and delegating. You will also be more time-effective if you tackle jobs which require mental effort when you feel at your best and able to concentrate; in other words when you are in the eustress zone. Do the tasks requiring less mental effort when you are not able to concentrate as well or when you anticipate interruptions. Do not waste time worrying unnecessarily about future events. *Remember, it's not the hours you put in – it's what you put into the hours that counts.*

Balancing your time between family, leisure, work and sleep is important. Regularly spending long periods at work will inevitably mean less time for your family and for leisure activities. Too much work often leads to mental fatigue and difficulty in relaxing, which will inevitably affect the quality of the time spent with your family and friends. Finding time to spend with your partner, children, family and friends will enable you to nurture love and support and to enhance your self-esteem and happiness.

Include in your daily schedule periods for relaxation, exercise and time for you to spend on your own. Pamper yourself each day. Build 'idling time' into your routine so as not to rush the things you do. Allow plenty of time for washing, dressing and eating breakfast even if it means rising half an hour earlier in the morning. Spend time on meditation and muscular relaxation. Allow more time than you estimate for journeys and give yourself time to be punctual for appointments. In this way, you will reduce anxiety if you are unexpectedly delayed.

Remember, there are 168 hours in each week so there is time to devote to everything; sit down and plan how you want to spend your time. Time is precious and we all want to spend it happily. So remember, for every 60 seconds you are angry you lose a minute of happiness.

ALLEVIATING YOUR EASILY AROUSED ANGER AND HOSTILITY
Question your Type A anger and hostility beliefs. Answer true or false to this statement: *'I need aggression and hostility to succeed'*. If your answer is 'true', then consider that by using aggression and hostility rather than understanding, you may damage your health and your relationships with family, friends and work colleagues. In the long run, this will not lead to success.

Making mistakes, failing to achieve goals, receiving adverse criticism, particularly in front of others, and perceiving a situation as unfair or embarrassing can trigger frustration and anger. As we described earlier, such emotion leads to excessive release of noradrenaline, the potential killer. When you next feel yourself getting irritated, aggravated and angry remember that, if triggered, your anger can inflict the most damage on the person you least intend – yourself. Train yourself to avoid anger: do not get hooked, practise anger control and use the quieting reflex (see page 142).

Try these two techniques: avoiding the hook and anger control.

Avoiding the hook
Picture yourself as a fish in a river. Every morning you wake up and start swimming. The waters ahead appear clear but on the banks of the river are anglers casting their hooks, hoping to catch you. Suddenly a worm on a hook appears in front of you. The bait looks tempting but if you bite you will be hooked. Think: 'Bite or pass by?' You pass by, avoiding the bait. Unexpectedly another hook drops in front of you. Ask yourself; 'Bite or pass by?' You pass by, only to find more hooks appearing along your journey.

Type As bite all the time, perhaps 30 to 40 times a day. The problem is that we have no idea when the next hook is going to appear and this makes anger and hostility difficult to deal with.

Insight
If you take the bait you will get hooked!

Anger control
If you feel yourself starting to take the bait, then say 'stop'. Detach yourself from the situation and analyse your behaviour and feelings. Ask yourself, 'What provoked me?' Identify the causes of your anger and the beliefs, attitudes and feelings that led you to take the bait. Now replay the situation again in your mind to see whether the way in which you acted was appropriate, justified and rational. Usually you will find taking the bait serves no real purpose. Remain calm and hold a conversation with yourself (called 'self-talk'): 'It's not worth getting worked up about'; 'There is no real reason to argue'; 'Keep cool, don't take the bait'; 'Unpleasantness can lead to more unpleasantness'; 'Practise QR'; 'Reason it out'.

The trick is not to take the bait and therefore not to get angry in the first place. Do not get hooked into things you cannot do anything about. So if the train is delayed and you are late for your appointment, use self-talk to accept that there is nothing you can do to make up the lost time. Instead use your energy to think about alleviating the problem. When you arrive at the station, telephone your appointment, explain the situation and say you will be arriving as soon as possible. You also have little control over the errors and antics of others, so learn to accept their mistakes and trivialities. If you cannot, this will inevitably lead to frustration, anger and hostility.

Work at lessening your sense of time urgency. Impatience is a mild form of irritation which in turn is a mild form of anger. Above all, recognize that your anger and hostility are manifestations of your low self-esteem. When self-esteem is high, then anger and hostility will be low. Blows to your self-esteem will easily trigger hostility, so work toward enhancing your self-esteem and practise being assertive. Note that your self-esteem is affected by the degree of love and affection in your life, so when love and affection are present, self-esteem will be high and the potential for hostility will be low. Learning to give and receive love and affection is therefore vital in your battle against anger and hostility. Tell your partner and children how much you value their love, affection and support and express your feelings to them. Take an interest in your friends and share their ups and downs. Also, learn to laugh at yourself and your mistakes and errors. Stop taking yourself too seriously!

For once, it is better to be in the 'B' team rather than the 'A' team.

14

Improving personal life skills

In this chapter you will learn:
- *the importance of life skills to stress and its management*
- *the power of love and support in managing stress*
- *techniques for improving personal life skills.*

Increasing love and support

Insight

The importance of love and support in helping you deal with distress cannot be emphasized strongly enough.

A considerable amount of research has shown that those people with low love and social support succumb to health problems more easily than those with high levels of love and support. It is easy to see why if we remember the effects of stress hormones. When a person feels secure, loved and well supported, noradrenaline, adrenaline and cortisol levels are all normal.

In discussing love and support, we intend this to be interpreted in its broadest sense. This includes not only our intimate relationships but also affection and respect between friends and support at work from colleagues.

WITHIN THE FAMILY

Love is one of our basic needs. From the cradle we yearn to be cuddled, hugged and kissed, particularly when we face the pressures and demands of growing up. Lack of love and affection or feeling unwanted often leads to problems in later life particularly when it comes to courtship, sexual relationships and parenting.

Love and support within the family is naturally our first experience. The parent–child relationship is crucial in moulding the future life of the child. Being unloved during childhood, conflict with parents and jealousy of affection and love given to brothers and sisters but not to them, is often the hallmark of a depressed person possessing a variety of psychological problems, and usually a bottle of tranquillizers.

In adulthood, touching, stroking and caressing are essential in developing relationships. Under the right circumstances, this is undoubtedly the best way to relax, reduce tension and therefore reduce distress. The direct power of this on our health is difficult to investigate, but stroking has been shown to be extremely therapeutic and has great impact on our wellbeing and health.

Those living alone but with a pet have been shown to have lower blood pressure, a lower incidence of sudden cardiac death and quicker recovery rates following operations than non-pet owners who live alone. Heart attack victims with pets tend to live longer than those who do not own a pet. Having a pet provides the opportunity for stroking, and a sense of belonging and not feeling isolated.

An experiment designed to investigate dietary fat intake and arterial disease in rabbits unexpectedly provided a good illustration of the powers of touching, stroking and affection. The researchers found that although all rabbits in the experiment were fed the same high-fat diet and lived in the same conditions, a small number failed to develop significant arterial disease. No reason could be found until it was realized that this particular group of rabbits was cared for by a technician who regularly stroked and cuddled each rabbit. Rabbits not receiving this treatment all developed significant arterial disease. So amazed were the researchers when they realized that cuddling and stroking might have this effect that they set up an experiment to test it. They repeated the original experiment but this time deliberately included the cuddling and stroking in one group of rabbits. The result was the same as in the first experiment. Those animals receiving physical attention developed very little coronary heart disease.

So do not underestimate the power and benefits of touching and caressing. Express your love and affection to your partner, children and family. Cuddle your partner or children while watching television (this is good polyphasing!). Respond to their signals of 'I want to be cuddled'. Too often the demands and pressures of work and parenting turn what were the exciting honeymoon years of marriage into a dreary relationship. When did you last say to your spouse, 'I love you'? When did you last buy your partner a small gift? Rekindle the courting years; ask your partner out to dinner next weekend and treat the occasion as your first date. Purchase a small gift for your partner, children or parents, or take your family out for a treat. Spend more time with them; so often we hear people's sadness and regrets over the lack of time given to their children.

IN FRIENDSHIP

The value of friendship is incalculable. It is not necessarily the number of friends you have that counts, but the quality of the friendship. One true friend is worth far more than several acquaintances. True friends share one another's interests and successes as well as failures. With a true friend, you can express yourself and be accepted for what and who you are. At work, mutual support between colleagues can be of tremendous help in getting the job done and reducing distress for everyone.

SHARING PROBLEMS

Family and friends should be people with whom you can share your problems, from whom to seek advice and sympathy. Undoubtedly one of the key values of love and support is being able to share and talk over problems with someone else. As the saying goes,

'A trouble shared is a trouble halved'. Talk over your problems at home and work, and help others by listening. Do not bottle things up inside; talk..., talk..., talk..., express your feelings to whomever you feel most comfortable and confident with.

Enhancing self-esteem

Self-esteem is the self-evaluation we make of our worth as a person. It is based on how competent, significant, likable and successful we think we are.

> **Insight**
> Feeling good about ourselves (high self-esteem) reduces distress and provides the platform for eustress, personal growth and development, effectiveness and creativity.

Our self-esteem is based largely on the relationship between our actual achievements and what we want and expect out of life. When achievements exceed expectations then self-esteem rises. On the other hand, failure to achieve expectations results in low self-esteem. This is where Type As find most of their problems; they set themselves never-ending and unrealistic targets and goals which they rarely achieve. As a result, they struggle to secure adequate self-esteem. Since Type As believe that self-esteem can be enhanced only by achieving, they set themselves yet more unattainable targets and goals. Failure is usually more frequent than success, so self-esteem is further lowered. A vicious circle is established.

When self-esteem is low the potential for anger and hostility is high. So when Type As fail to achieve their expectations, their self-esteem is lowered and they become frustrated, irritable, angry and hostile. Aggression is then used in an attempt to achieve the impossible.

Type Bs, on the other hand, have much more realistic expectations. As a result, their achievements often surpass their expectations so self-esteem is rarely dented and remains secure.

One of the most difficult things in life is to discover yourself and to set yourself realistic goals and expectations which you feel able to achieve. You may need to be content with achieving less than 100 per cent.

Praise and recognition for a job well done is guaranteed to raise self-esteem. This is a good management strategy for establishing and maintaining a happy and productive workforce. With self-esteem high, cooperation is more likely. When dealing with others, remember that their self-esteem is easily damaged by adverse criticism of their work, mistakes and shortcomings. Also, praise yourself for a task well done by using self-talk.

Changing your self-image (how you see yourself) means reviewing all aspects of your life. Accept your faults and insecurities and work to resolve them. Harness your strengths and capitalize on them. Do not try to be what you feel others want you to be; be honest with yourself and others. Express yourself; grow beyond what you are.

Looking good, feeling healthy, fit and loved, smiling, developing a sense of humour, not taking life or yourself too seriously and being assertive are all self-esteem boosters.

Thinking positively

Think positively. You will gain more from life by thinking positively than by taking a cautious and negative approach. In other words, be an optimist rather than a pessimist. This will help reduce anxiety since pessimists often live with the fear of failure. For each situation you meet, you can be negative or positive. Look to the positive aspects and learn and gain something from everything you do.

Insight
When things go wrong, learn from your mistakes and do not dwell on your failures.

Each time you find yourself thinking negatively switch to positive thinking by using self-talk: 'It can't be this bad – there must be something I can gain from this situation.' By thinking positively, we reinforce our behaviours which protect us from self-destructive thoughts.

Learning to be assertive

Insight
Being assertive is a most effective way of increasing your coping resources.

Assertiveness is a way of communicating effectively. It means being able to say what you feel, think or want. It also means being able to understand other people's points of view and to negotiate and reach a workable compromise in awkward situations. Behaving assertively will boost your self-esteem and reduce anger and aggression.

We are all assertive to some degree. However, we can learn to be more effective communicators. Here is an example of assertiveness:

A work colleague asks to borrow your book. You know this person has a reputation for never returning borrowed material. Your assertive response might be:

'I realize that you need material from this book.'

This lets the other person know that you heard, understood and acknowledge their request. You then say:

'However, I do not like to lend my books.'

This states how you feel or what you think. You finally add:

'I suggest that you try the library, I know they have a copy.'

By this statement, you are making some recommendations. You let the other person know that you want to help by making constructive suggestions.

Your first statement, 'I realize that you need material from this book', tells the other person that you acknowledge what is being said and that you understand what they are saying. This statement should begin with a phrase such a 'I understand' or 'I realize' or 'I appreciate'. When you get into the habit of using this approach, you will find yourself listening to (not just hearing) what someone is saying. This is a good drill for modifying Type A Behaviour.

Your second statement should always start with the word 'However'. Never say 'but' because this is an aggressive word. Now you need to express your feelings about this issue. State clearly what you feel or think... 'I do not like to lend my books'. You have to be honest with yourself and this takes courage. Everyone has the right to say how they feel. By being honest you will feel better afterwards. This will also help raise your self-esteem and increase self-respect and self-confidence. There is no suppression or bottling-up of emotions, so the potential for activating your stress response is decreased and there is less chance of hostility. Again, a good drill for reducing Type A Behaviour and learning to say 'no'!

The third statement, 'I suggest that you try the library, I know they have a copy', should be a constructive suggestion on what to do about the situation. You must state what you want or what action you want taken. It is important to be positive and this may lead to negotiating and arriving at a workable compromise. Starting this statement with one of the following phrases is useful:

▶ *'I'd prefer it if...'*
▶ *'I suggest that...'*
▶ *'I'd appreciate it if...'*

and so on. It is important not to become aggressive here – do not tell the other person to 'get lost' or words to that effect. You must provide them with a constructive suggestion.

Notice that the above example illustrates a reasonable, rational answer. This is what being assertive is all about – being reasonable. If you are reasonable then the other person is less likely to take offence. You have shown this person that you appreciate what is being asked, you have explained how you feel about the matter and you have been helpful. In other words, you have been assertive! Communication has been effective, progress has been made, you have responded in a Type B manner and you have handled the situation appropriately with no distress to yourself.

What if the other person becomes insistent or aggressive about your assertive response? In this case, you simply repeat your previous comments, keeping to the three steps:

- ▶ *understand…*
- ▶ *however…*
- ▶ *suggest…*

This way you will eventually arrive at a workable solution. With practice, you will gain confidence in being assertive and this will take much of the distress out of life.

On some occasions, you may find that being assertive does not do the trick. It may be that a source of conflict remains unresolved no matter how assertive you are. It is important not to become too upset about this and not to blame yourself or others, otherwise your confidence will be undermined. Instead, try to look upon your situation positively and use self-talk, as described in the section on anger control (page 195). When you find that, by being assertive, you have solved a problem successfully, then congratulate yourself by self-talk. Praising yourself in this way will also show you the value of praising others.

Smiling, laughing and developing a sense of humour

It may be a strange thing to say, but many people appear to have lost the ability to smile. Just look around you to see what we mean.

A genuine facial smile should reflect a 'smile' from your heart. Seeing someone smile will usually make you smile. Smiling makes you feel happy.

This is probably because smiling relaxes many of the facial muscles, thereby improving blood flow to the brain. More facial muscles are used for frowning and in anger than when smiling. Look in the mirror, screw your face up in angry grimaces and look at how many muscles you are using. Now smile. You will see that far fewer muscles are used as you smile.

Learn to avoid going about your daily activities with a worried or angry look on your face. Smile instead; you not only feel better but others relate to you more easily. So start the day with a 'heartfelt' smile. Smiling is a good way of coping with stress and reducing irritation, anger and hostility. Joking and laughter can defuse tense and awkward situations.

The British Safety Council recognizes the benefits of smiling and laughter in reducing accident-proneness and in improving work performance. They actually hold a 'Smile for Safety' week. A recent study has shown that humour at work eases mental tension, aids concentration and enhances creativity. No wonder some companies now hold humour workshops for their employees.

Insight
Laughter and humour can have a powerful effect on the mind and body.

The story of Norman Cousins illustrates this point. Almost crippled by an incurable disease, he decided to take his treatment into his own hands. He read humorous books, sought out jokes and watched comedy films. After a short time he recovered sufficiently to return to work. Norman put his recovery down to 'laughter therapy'. At the time there was much scepticism about his claim but today many researchers and doctors believe that laughter can induce changes in body activity that improve the circulation and digestion and reduce muscle tension. One of the most interesting findings is that laughter increases the number of cells of the immune system that help to prevent infection, hence improving our immune function. Furthermore, studies have shown that some cancer patients who have more of these immune system cells have a better prognosis. So laughter may well be the best medicine, as Norman Cousins found. In fact, many of the effects are the opposite to those seen in distress. So, perhaps we should include laughter sessions in our daily routine.

It is important that we learn to laugh at ourselves. Widows of heart attack victims often report that their partners had lost their sense of humour and the ability to laugh at themselves. People who have a sense of humour have learned to laugh at themselves and not to take life too seriously. In fact, a sense of humour is high on the list of what we look for in other people when forming relationships.

No wonder it is said that laughter is the best medicine.

15

Your personal stress management plan

In this chapter you will learn:
- *how to develop a personal stress management plan*
- *how to implement your plan*
- *how to monitor, evaluate and revise your plan.*

How to prepare for a personal stress management plan is covered in Chapter 8. Preparation also involves reading Part two and Part three of this book. Please read these before you commence working and implementing your personal stress management plan.

Your personal SMP is designed to make you to think about tackling significant stressors in your life, including your views, beliefs and expectations about life. You have chosen *three key stressors* as representing significant events, objects or situations, either distressful or eustressful. Now is there something that can be done about them? This is where thought and planning may help to diminish their effects over time, and prevent them from taking on major significance again. This chapter guides you through a programme of self-help. It involves a four-point framework:

1 *Thinking about technique(s) which can help to get a handle on a stressor.*
2 *Practising a possible technique(s) by bringing it into your lifestyle as part of your daily routine.*

3   *Evaluating on a regular basis* the impact of your chosen technique(s) for each of your significant stressors.
4   *Revising your choice of techniques* as necessary until your significant stressors become insignificant, i.e. until your signs and symptoms score is reduced.

Remember: Think, Practise, Evaluate and Revise: TPER

Your SMP is designed as a 12-week programme (from day 1 to day 85). However, it does not mean that after 12 weeks everything finishes. In fact, it is intended that after 12 weeks you may be making sufficient progress that you do not need to keep referring back to the plan; you just carry on with the good work as part of a modified lifestyle and new you.

If, however, you find that the SMP is not working, it may be that the techniques need reviewing. You may need to follow up on other techniques, or you may need more guidance. We have provided a reading list (page 241) and some useful websites (page 243) so that you can explore further afield. The important point is to remember the basis of our four-point SMP: TPER: think about techniques, practise them (give it time), evaluate their impact, revise as appropriate. *Do not give up.* Stress management is continuous, involving continued learning and refinement. It can take an entire lifetime to achieve. A summary of the procedure in the form of a diary is shown on page 211. It will be useful for reference in monitoring and evaluating your progress.

How to develop your stress management plan

First make six copies each of Figure 15.3 Stress management plan evaluation (page 212) and Figure 15.4 Revised stress management plan (page 213). Keep these tables in a folder to complete as you undertake your SMP. They will also provide a useful source of reference if you need to revise your plan.

DAY 0: TACKLING YOUR THREE KEY STRESSORS

Before you can implement your SMP, you need to devise a way of dealing with your three key stressors. This will be the aim of your SMP. To do this, first of all focus on possible stress management techniques that you feel may help to deal with each of your three key stressors. Identify up to six techniques that you feel you would prefer to use and write them in Figure 15.1.

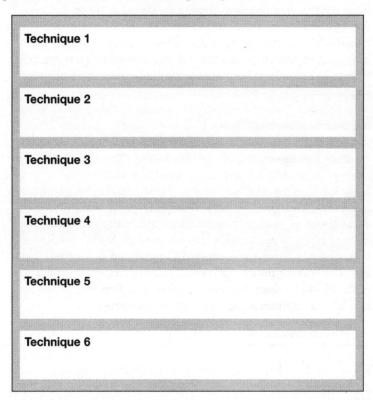

Figure 15.1 My chosen stress management techniques.

Now consider each of your three key stressors (from Figure 8.3 on page 114) in turn. In Figure 15.2 write out how you plan to tackle each key stressor, by using one or more of the techniques which you have chosen (in Figure 15.1). Think about how you can put these techniques into action. You may find it helpful to refer to your responses from the coping ability self-assessment on page 119 when choosing your techniques. Items 1 to 9 reflect helpful techniques for dealing effectively with stress, so focus on enhancing those where you answered 'Yes' and strive to achieve those where you answered 'No'. Items 10 to 15, however, reflect inappropriate techniques for dealing with stress. Select techniques to change your lifestyle for those items where you have answered 'Yes'.

You may need to use more than one technique for each stressor. Also you may decide to use the same technique for more than one of your key stressors. If you think your selected techniques seem inappropriate for your key stressors, then refer back to the variety of techniques described in Chapters 9 to 14 to select one that you feel may be more suitable.

Plan for stressor 1

Plan for stressor 2

Plan for stressor 3

Date for evaluation of stress management plan:
Day 14:

Figure 15.2 My stress management plan – Day 0: Date:

DAY 1: IMPLEMENTING YOUR STRESS MANAGEMENT PLAN

When you are satisfied with your choice of technique for each key stressor, you are ready to implement your SMP. Remember TPER: think, practise, evaluate, revise.

Start practising each of the techniques you have chosen for each of your key stressors. *Practise these for two weeks.*

Follow the suggested 12-week programme set out as a summary diary below. Develop your plan on Day 0 (Sunday) and start practising the SMP on Day 1 (Monday).

On Day 14 (Sunday) assess your progress (see page 212).

Summary diary	
Day 0: Sunday: (date:	) Develop SMP
Day 1 to 13:	Practise SMP
Day 14: Sunday: (date:	) Evaluate and revise SMP
Day 15 to 28:	Practise SMP
Day 29: Sunday: (date:	) Evaluate and revise SMP
Day 30 to 42:	Practise SMP
Day 43: Sunday: (date:	) Evaluate and revise SMP
Day 44 to 56:	Practise SMP
Day 57: Sunday: (date:	) Evaluate and revise SMP
Day 58 to 70:	Practise SMP
Day 71: Sunday: (date:	) Evaluate and revise SMP
Day 72 to 84:	Practise SMP
Day 85: Sunday: (date:	) Evaluate and revise SMP and 12-week self-assessment

How to evaluate and revise your stress management plan

DAY 14: EVALUATING AND REVISING YOUR STRESS MANAGEMENT PLAN

Day 14 (Sunday) is the time to assess your progress. Look at the plans (in Figure 15.2) for each of your key stressors. Ask yourself 'In which ways have the techniques used in the SMP helped or hindered?' Make a note in Figure 15.3 below, of any factors that have contributed to helping, or that have been unhelpful, for each key stressor.

Plan evaluation for stressor 1

Plan evaluation for stressor 2

Plan evaluation for stressor 3

Figure 15.3 Stress management plan evaluation – Day: Date:

Now look at what you have written and consider your techniques.

Continue to practise those techniques that seem to be making a difference. For those that are unhelpful, think about your SMP for the key stressor concerned. It may be that the technique needs to be practised for longer. Remember, for example, that effective modification of Type A Behaviour requires drilling over a period of at least eight weeks. Also, active relaxation techniques need a minimum of six weeks before becoming beneficial. So try to give the chosen technique a chance of becoming effective.

On the other hand if you find a technique unacceptable, rethink your SMP for the key stressor concerned. Write out in Figure 15.4 how you intend to continue, with a revised SMP. Which technique(s) will you use for each key stressor? Your revised SMP may include most of the same information that you already have in your SMP for Day 1 (Figure 15.2). This is fine. Keep all of your tables to monitor and evaluate your progress.

Revised plan for stressor 1
Revised plan for stressor 2
Revised plan for stressor 3
To be evaluated on Day: Date

Figure 15.4 Revised stress management plan – Day: Date:

When you are satisfied with your revised SMP, practise *all* your techniques (new and original) for each of your three key stressors. Do this until your next evaluation which is on day 29.

DAY 29: EVALUATING AND REVISING YOUR STRESS MANAGEMENT PLAN

On Day 29 evaluate your revised SMP from Day 14 (Figure 15.4). Ask yourself 'In which ways have the techniques used in the SMP helped or hindered?'

Make a note in a blank copy of Figure 15.3 of any factors that have contributed to helping or hindering you in dealing with each of your key stressors.

Now look at what you have written and consider your techniques. Continue to practise those techniques that seem to be making a difference. For those that are unhelpful, think about your SMP for the key stressor concerned. It may be that the techniques need reviewing. You may need to follow up on other techniques. We have provided a reading list so that you can explore further afield. Or you may need more guidance. Again, our resource base at the back of this book can point you in the right direction.

On the other hand if you find a technique unacceptable, rethink your SMP for the key stressor concerned. Write out in a blank copy of Figure 15.4 how you intend to continue with a revised SMP. Which technique(s) will you use for each key stressor?

When you are satisfied with your revised SMP, continue with the implementation – practise your techniques. Carry on practising until Day 43. On Day 43 assess your progress and revise your SMP as before.

Repeat the process of evaluating and revising your SMP, every two weeks, as shown in the summary diary using the blank copies of Figures 15.3 and 15.4 that you copied earlier.

DAY 85: REPEAT SELF-ASSESSMENT

How successful has your SMP been? Now that you have practised your techniques to deal with your three key stressors, you are ready to reassess your signs and symptoms, Type A Behaviour, work attitude, work stress and coping ability. This will also be an opportunity to recheck your life events, although in such a relatively short period these will most likely be unchanged. Complete all the self-assessment questionnaires that follow.

RE-ASSESSMENT OF SIGNS AND SYMPTOMS

Tick the most appropriate box.

During the last month have you:	(a) Almost never	(b) Some-times	(c) Most of the time	(d) Almost all the time
1 been easily irritated by people or trivial events?	❏	❏	❏	❏
2 felt impatient?	❏	❏	❏	❏
3 felt unable to cope?	❏	❏	❏	❏
4 felt a failure?	❏	❏	❏	❏
5 found it difficult to make decisions?	❏	❏	❏	❏
6 lost interest in other people?	❏	❏	❏	❏
7 felt you had no one to confide in or to talk to about your problems?	❏	❏	❏	❏
8 found it difficult to concentrate?	❏	❏	❏	❏
9 failed to finish tasks/jobs before moving on to the next, leaving jobs incomplete?	❏	❏	❏	❏
10 felt neglected in any way?	❏	❏	❏	❏
11 tried to do too many things at once?	❏	❏	❏	❏
12 felt anxious or depressed?	❏	❏	❏	❏
13 been uncharacteristically aggressive?	❏	❏	❏	❏
14 felt bored?	❏	❏	❏	❏
15 changed your patterns of drinking, smoking or eating?	❏	❏	❏	❏
16 changed your level of sexual activity?	❏	❏	❏	❏
17 cried or had the desire to cry?	❏	❏	❏	❏
18 felt tired most of the time?	❏	❏	❏	❏
19 suffered from any of the following more frequently – back and neck pain, headaches, muscular aches and pains, muscular spasms and cramps, constipation, diarrhoea, loss of appetite, heartburn, indigestion and nausea?	❏	❏	❏	❏
20 Do two or more of the following apply to you – bite your nails, clench your fists, drum your fingers, grind your teeth, hunch your shoulders, tap your feet, have trouble falling or staying asleep?	❏	❏	❏	❏
Total				

For scoring turn to page 225. Make a note of your score in the table on page 221.

RE-ASSESSMENT OF TYPE A BEHAVIOUR

For each question tick the box that best represents your behaviour.

	Never	Almost never	Some-times	Usually	Almost always	Always
Are you late for appointments?	❑	❑	❑	❑	❑	❑
Are you competitive; in the games you play at home or at work?	❑	❑	❑	❑	❑	❑
In conversations do you anticipate what others are going to say (head nod, interrupt, finish sentences for them)?	❑	❑	❑	❑	❑	❑
Do you have to do things in a hurry?	❑	❑	❑	❑	❑	❑
Do you get impatient in queues or traffic jams?	❑	❑	❑	❑	❑	❑
Do you try to do several things at once and think about what you are about to do next?	❑	❑	❑	❑	❑	❑
Do you feel you do most things quickly (eating, waking, talking, driving)?	❑	❑	❑	❑	❑	❑
Do you get easily irritated over trivia?	❑	❑	❑	❑	❑	❑
If you make a mistake, do you get angry with yourself?	❑	❑	❑	❑	❑	❑
Do you find fault with and criticize other people?	❑	❑	❑	❑	❑	❑
Total						

For scoring and evaluation turn to page 225. When you have calculated your score write this in the table on page 221.

RE-ASSESSMENT OF YOUR ATTITUDE TO WORK – WORKAHOLISM

	Yes	No
Do you take work home most nights?	☐	☐
Do you frequently think about work problems at home?	☐	☐
Do you voluntarily work long hours?	☐	☐
Do work problems affect your sleeping habits?	☐	☐
Do your family and friends complain that you spend too little time with them?	☐	☐
Do you find it difficult to relax and forget work?	☐	☐
Do you find it difficult to say 'no' to work requests?	☐	☐
Do you find it difficult to delegate?	☐	☐
Is your self-esteem based largely on your work?	☐	☐
Score		

Turn to page 226 for scoring and evaluation. Write your score in the table on page 221.

RE-ASSESSMENT OF IDENTIFYING STRESS AT WORK

This questionnaire is a guide to help identify stressors at work. For each aspect of your job write the stress rating to indicate how much stress you experience. Add your scores and write the total in the box.

Stress rating
0 = no stress
1 = slightly stressful
2 = moderately stressful
3 = very stressful
4 = extremely stressful

For scoring and evaluation turn to page 228. Write your score in the table on page 221.

Aspects of your job	Stress rating
The physical conditions at work, e.g. ventilation, noise, lighting, heating	☐
The freedom to choose your work	☐
The freedom to get on with your work your colleagues	☐
The recognition you get for good work	☐
Having more than one immediate boss	☐
Your immediate boss or bosses	☐
The amount of responsibility you are given	☐
Your rate of pay	☐
Your opportunity to use your abilities	☐
Industrial relations between management and workers in your organization	☐
Your chance of promotion	☐
the way your organization is managed	☐
The attention paid to suggestions you make	☐
The number of hours worked	☐
The amount of variety in your job	☐
he security of your employment	☐
Any other aspect	☐
Total score	☐

RE-ASSESSMENT OF LIFE EVENTS

Tick off the listed events which you have experienced during the last 12 months, then turn to page 227 to check your list against the scores for each item. Write your score in the box for each item and then add up the scores. Write your score in the table on page 221.

	tick	score		tick	score
Death of a partner	☐	___	Child leaves home	☐	___
Divorce	☐	___	Trouble with in-laws	☐	___
Separation from partner	☐	___	Outstanding personal achievement	☐	___
Jail sentence	☐	___	Partner begins or stops work	☐	___
Death of a close family member	☐	___	Child begins or ends school	☐	___
Injury or illness to yourself	☐	___	Change in living conditions	☐	___
Marriage – your own	☐	___	Change of personal habits	☐	___
Given the sack at work	☐	___	Trouble with boss or employer	☐	___
Reconciliation with partner	☐	___	Change in working hours and conditions	☐	___
Retirement	☐	___	Change in residence	☐	___
Ill health in member of family	☐	___	Child changes schools	☐	___
Pregnancy – your own	☐	___	Change in recreation	☐	___
Sexual problems/difficulties	☐	___	Change in church activities	☐	___
Addition of new family member	☐	___	Change in social activities	☐	___
Major business or work changes	☐	___	Take on a small mortgage or loan	☐	___
Change in your financial state	☐		Change in sleeping habits	☐	___
Death of a friend	☐	—	Change in number of family get-togethers	☐	___
Change to a different type of work	☐	___	Change in eating habits	☐	___
More arguments with partner	☐	___	Holiday	☐	___
Take on a large mortgage	☐	___	Christmas (coming soon)	☐	___
Mortgage or loan foreclosed	☐	___	Minor violations of the law	☐	___
Change in responsibilities at work	☐	___	Total score		[____]

This scale is adapted from Holmes and Rahe's Life Change Index, *Journal of Psychosomatic Research*, 1967 Vol. 11.

RE-ASSESSMENT OF COPING ABILITY

	Tick either Yes or No.	Yes	No
1	Do you have supportive family/friends?	❏	❏
2	Do you have a hobby?	❏	❏
3	Do you belong to a social or activity group?	❏	❏
4	Do you practise an active relaxation technique (yoga, meditation, imagery, autogenic training, etc.) on a daily basis?	❏	❏
5	Do you exercise for at least 20 minutes three times a week?	❏	❏
6	Do you do something 'just for yourself' each week that you really enjoy?	❏	❏
7	Do you have somewhere you can go in order to be alone?	❏	❏
8	Have you attended a stress management, relaxation, time management or assertiveness training course?	❏	❏
9	Do you show Type B behaviour?	❏	❏
10	Do you smoke?	❏	❏
11	Do you drink alcohol to relax?	❏	❏
12	Do you take sleeping pills?	❏	❏
13	Do you take work home?	❏	❏
14	Do you drink more than eight cups of caffeinated drinks (coffee, tea, coke, chocolate) each day?	❏	❏
15	Do you show Type A behaviour?	❏	❏
	Total		

For scoring and evaluation turn to page 229. Make a note of your total score in the table on page 221.

ASSESSMENT OF YOUR PROGRESS ON DAY 85

Compare your Day 85 scores with your initial scores.

Summary of self-assessment	Date:	
	Initial score	Score Day 85
Signs and symptoms (pages 62 and 215)	☐	☐
Type A Behaviour (pages 92 and 216)	☐	☐
Your attitude to work (pages 99 and 217)	☐	☐
Life events (pages 103 and 219)	☐	☐
Identifying stress at work (pages 106 and 217)	☐	☐
Coping ability (pages 120 and 220)	☐	☐

HOW SUCCESSFUL HAS YOUR SMP BEEN?

Check your progress below.

Day 85 score lower in any of:	Day 85 score higher in:	
Signs and symptoms Type A Behaviour Work attitude Identifying stress at work	Coping	} Successful SMP

Your SMP appears to be working and as a result your health, work performance and relationships are likely to have improved. Continue to practise your SMP.

Day 85 score unchanged or higher in any of:	Day 85 score unchanged or lower in:	Unsuccessful SMP
Signs and symptoms		
Type A Behaviour	Coping	
Work attitude		
Identifying stress at work		

You may not be dealing well with your demands and pressures and as a result your health, work performance and relationships may suffer. We suggest you go back and work through the SMP again. It may help if you recruit someone to support you as you work through the plan.

Learning new skills to deal effectively with pressures and demands is not easy and can take a considerable time. You may need to find the time for this. Tackle only two or three stressors at a time and do not rush. Eventually you will find effective techniques to deal with your stressors. Reducing your stressors a few at a time and, at the same time, building up your general coping skills, will gradually lead to managing your stress effectively.

After Day 85, start your SMP programme again to deal with another three key stressors. Keep repeating this programme to deal with your stressors as and when they arise.

Always keep a check on your life events score and level of work stressors. Remember that if your life events score increases, your body and mind are being taxed more. In this case you will need to concentrate on developing your general coping skills.

Monitoring your work stressors will provide an indication of the added pressures and demands you need to cope with.

Finally...

Remember that this stress management plan is meant to act as a guide to help you focus on particular aspects of your circumstances that you may not have otherwise considered. We must point out that most of our distress results from our interactions with others, and that in this book we cannot prescribe individual tailor-made solutions. Each of us has to work on our own stress management plan according to our own individual situation. We wish you success in managing stress and being wise about your stress.

10 THINGS TO REMEMBER FROM CHAPTERS 13 AND 14

1 *Avoid activating your stress response when it is not needed.*

2 *Type As, through their beliefs, attitudes and habits, frequently perceive situations as threatening and challenging when no real threat or challenge exists.*

3 *Most of us display some degree of Type A Behaviour so we can all benefit from taking a more Type B approach to life.*

4 *Place a heart on your steering wheel or dashboard as a reminder to rid yourself of Type A driving habits.*

5 *Take time to look around to see what pleasurable things can be found.*

6 *If you take the bait you will get hooked!*

7 *The importance of love and support in helping you deal with distress cannot be emphasized strongly enough.*

8 *Feeling good about ourselves (high self-esteem) reduces distress and provides the platform for eustress, personal growth and development, effectiveness and creativity.*

9 *Learn from your mistakes and do not dwell on your failures.*

10 *Being assertive is an effective way of increasing coping resources.*

Appendix I: Scoring and evaluation

Signs and symptoms

SCORING

Questions 1, 5, 7, 8, 14, 16, 17 and 18
    Score (d) 6 (c) 4 (b) 2 (a) 0
Questions 2, 6, 9, 10, 11, 15, 19 and 20
    Score (d) 3 (c) 2 (b) 1 (a) 0
Questions 3, 4, 12 and 13
    Score (d) 30 (c) 20 (b) 10 (a) 0

Evaluation
If your score is over 30, then you are most likely to be suffering from distress. The higher you score towards the maximum of 192 the more distress you are suffering. Scores of over 60 are a cause for concern and indicate that you should discuss your lifestyle with your doctor.

Type A Behaviour

SCORE

5 = Always   2 = Sometimes
4 = Almost always   1 = Almost never
3 = Usually   0 = Never

Total your scores and multiply by 2.

Evaluation

Type B	0–39	You are slightly and/or rarely impatient and aggravated. You create hardly any unnecessary stress for yourself and your health is probably unaffected.
Mild Type A	40–59	You are fairly and/or occasionally impatient and aggravated. You create some unnecessary stress for yourself and this may affect your health.
Moderate Type A	60–79	You are very and/or often impatient and aggravated. You generate much unnecessary stress for yourself and this may affect your health.
Extreme Type A	80–100	You are extremely and/or usually impatient and aggravated. You generate *too much* unnecessary stress for yourself and this may affect your health.

NOTE: This is a self-assessment of your Type A Behaviour. It is only as accurate as you are honest in your answers. Furthermore Type As are often blind to their own behaviour: for example, doing things fast. Type As may not think they are as fast as they actually are.

Your attitude to work – workaholism

Your score equals the number of 'yes' responses.

SCORING AND EVALUATION

Score: 1
If you answer 'yes' to one question you may simply be dedicated to your work. However, there is a fine dividing line between

dedication and obsessive devotion to work (workaholism) so be on your guard!

Score: 2
If you answer 'yes' to two questions you are obsessive about your work and could easily succumb to workaholism. Beware!

Answering 'yes' to more than two questions indicates you have an obsessive and compulsive devotion to work. The higher the score the more you are hooked into workaholism. You need to question your priorities for the sake of your marriage, social relationships, health and career; it may seem hard for you to believe you can be damaging the career that you are striving obsessively to enhance.

Life events

SCORE

Death of partner	100	Child leaves home	29
Divorce	73	Trouble with in-laws	29
Separation from partner	65	Outstanding personal achievement	28
Jail sentence	63	Partner begins or stops work	26
Death of a close family member	63	Child begins or ends school	26
Injury or illness to yourself	53	Change in living conditions	25
Marriage – your own	50	Change of personal habits	24
Given the sack at work	47	Trouble with boss or employer	23
Reconciliation with partner	45	Change in working hours and conditions	20
Retirement	45	Change in residence	20
Ill health in member of family	44	Child changes schools	20
Pregnancy – your own	40	Change in recreation	19
Sexual problems/ difficulties	39	Change in church activities	19

Addition of new family member	39	Change in social activities	18
Major business or work changes	39	Take on a small mortgage or loan	17
Change in your financial state	38	Change in sleeping habits	16
Death of a friend	37	Change in number of family get-togethers	15
Change to a different type of work	36	Change in eating habits	15
More arguments with partner	35	Holiday	13
Take on a large mortgage	31	Christmas (coming soon)	12
Mortgage or loan foreclosed	30	Minor violations of the law	11
Change in responsibilities at work	29		

Evaluation

Your risk of illness during the next two years if you score 300 or more is 80 per cent; for a score of 150–299 it is 50 per cent; for a score of 100–149 it is 30 per cent. Less than 100 indicates no change in risk.

Identifying stress at work

SCORE

Below 21: Your job does not appear to cause you too much distress.

21 to 40: It appears that your job may be the source of some distress.

41 to 60: Your job appears to be a cause of much distress.

Above 60: Your job appears to be a major source of distress.

Coping ability

SCORE

Points

1	yes	score 20	--------
2	yes	score 10	--------
3	yes	score 5 (if you attend more than once a month score 10)	--------
4	yes	score 15	--------
5	yes	score 10	--------
6	yes	score 10	--------
7	yes	score 10	--------
8	yes	score 10 for each course attended	--------
9	yes	score 15	--------

Total score for good coping strategies:

10	yes	subtract 10 points for each pack of 20 cigarettes smoked each day	--------
11	yes	subtract 10 points for every eight units drunk each week above the recommended limits shown on page 166	--------
12	yes	subtract 10	--------
13	yes	subtract 5 points for each night of the week that you take work home	--------
14	yes	subtract 5 points for every five cups over eight cups per day	--------
15	yes	check your Type A Behaviour assessment. Subtract 5 points if you scored between 40 and 60; 10 points if you scored 60 to 70 and 15 points if you scored over 70	--------

Total score for poor coping strategies:

Coping ability score: Subtract your score for poor coping strategies from your score for good coping strategies:

Evaluation

A positive score indicates you have good coping ability – the higher your score the better your ability to deal with the pressures and demands you face.

A negative score indicates you have poor coping ability – the lower your score the lower your ability to deal with the pressures and demands you face.

Appendix II: Stress management techniques that affect the stress response

In this Appendix you will learn:

▶ *evidence-based stress response altering techniques*
▶ *how the techniques work*
▶ *what the benefits are of each technique.*

We have seen in Chapter 3 (see Figure 3.3) that activation of the stress response is really an appreciation of the ways in which stress ultimately affects our body organs. It follows that stress management techniques, that rebalance cortisol levels (see Chapter 3, Figure 3.6) and hence restore the body organs back towards the normal stress balance, are advantageous. Do such techniques exist? If so, it means that we have an objective basis by which we can monitor and assess the effectiveness of stress management.

Our knowledge and understanding is improving about the ways in which some stress management techniques operate.

Here, we review a number of stress management techniques about which there is a growing body of objective evidence for their mechanism of action and their effectiveness. These form the basis of a useful resource to apply in stress management planning:

▶ *cognitive behavioural therapy*
▶ *neuro linguistic programming*
▶ *hypnotherapy*
▶ *music therapy*
▶ *aromatherapy*
▶ *orthomolecular vitamin redox regimes.*

Cognitive behavioural therapy

Often referred to as CBT, this is a therapy to alter thought processes. It is a form of training to learn to change the way in which you think about yourself and about your relationship with others. Therapy provides a way of gradually altering attitude to a more balanced view of the world.

CBT originates from work by Albert Ellis in the 1950s on Rational Emotive Therapy (RET). According to Ellis, irrational and self-defeating thoughts are linked to emotional problems but can be corrected by replacing them with more rational thinking.

In the 1960s and 1970s, Aaron Beck developed what he called cognitive therapy which became known for its effective treatment of depression. He proposed that negative thoughts, originating from value systems learned from experiences as early as childhood, will lower mood. This sets a pattern of learning that increases the likelihood that further negative thinking will occur, resulting in a cycle that maintains low mood, producing cognitive distortions of reality and resulting in a general depressed influence over daily functioning.

Today, CBT has become the treatment of choice for most of those seeking psychotherapy. Through CBT, a person, with the help of a trained therapist, in a number of regular sessions, identifies and gains insight into their own unhelpful thoughts and beliefs that drive their behaviour. Therapy provides skills to effect changes, often permanent, in the style of thinking, for example, assertiveness training, conflict management, humour training, improved communication skills training, anxiety management training, relaxation training and problem solving. In order to achieve such changes, the person has to be ready, willing and able to effect changes in their own thinking. It requires work and commitment to effect the change. Success can lead to significant changes in attitude which can cause an appropriate stress response activation to get back, and stay, in the normal stress balance zone.

Neuro linguistic programming (NLP)

This is a course of training in which an individual learns to change their style of thinking, their feelings, language and behaviour by modelling on a particular high-achieving individual or individuals.

NLP emerged in the 1970s from work by John Grinder and Richard Bandler. They were interested in identifying human high achieving performance and 'excellence'. They produced models of language structure (communication) and behaviour (action response) of successful achievers, providing a basis on which to formulate models which mirror outstanding skills.

Grinder and Bandler went on to offer training courses for self-improvement. Such courses have been particularly popular in work-related fields of activity for example, team building, marketing, leadership training. The principles of NLP are also helpful in individual personal development generally, thereby having an overall potential to rebalance stress response activity.

A key element of NLP, with the help of a trainer, is to develop understanding about intrapersonal communication (how we see ourselves and how we have come to formulate such a mindset) as it relates to interpersonal communication (how we communicate with others and how our behaviour appears to others). This involves training courses to learn about individual mental image representation and formulation, and to learn to examine how this relates to the world around the individual and, in their interactions with others, how it affects performance. Training then involves modelling on the behaviour of successful, significant others to alter patterns of communication and behaviour for more effective performance.

Hypnotherapy

This is a therapy in which an individual learns to alter their unhelpful responses to a more balanced form, popularized by claims that almost any condition can be cured. It is used to treat a range of conditions including anxiety, addictions, phobias and pain. Recently, scientific interest has centred on two applications: in the management of irritable bowel syndrome and in the reduction of pain, for example, during surgical procedures without the use of a local or even a general anaesthetic. Research studies have shown that hypnosis, through the induction of a state of deep relaxation, leads to an overall decrease in cortisol secretion and an improvement in immune function.

Hypnosis appears to be manifested in an individual as a trance-like state. This is considered by some to be a state of altered consciousness in the form of highly focussed attention on internal thoughts and feelings with detachment from what is going on around in the immediate environment. This state is attained gradually, within about 30 minutes, through a trained hypnotherapist who first induces a state of deep relaxation, using verbal exercises. In the second half of the session, the therapist repeats a series of verbal suggestions, while the person is in a receptive state. The type of suggestions made depend on the condition that is being treated and on the training and preferences of the therapist. There is no standardized format to the procedure.

Sometimes, one session is sufficient but usually several sessions are required to establish learning patterns in the recipient that decrease the likelihood of negative or undesired thinking or behaviour recurring and resulting in desired patterns of responding.

Music therapy

Rhythmic sounds produce a brainwave activity that brings about a feeling of calmness and physical relaxation. The effect of rhythmic music, ritual drumming and chanting on the human state of mind has been used for centuries. Today, neuroscientists are exploring the power of music on brain activity as a way to influence disease processes and to treat mental illness. A new field of study has emerged – music therapy. We can harness the power of music to manage stress.

Most of us will already have experienced how music can change our thinking and affect our emotions. Film music creates an atmosphere of excitement, tenseness, horror, danger, serenity and love. Lullabies at bedtime induce sleep in children. We appreciate that slow, melodic, repetitive and soft music can bring about a state of calmness, whereas loud heavy rock can raise alertness, arousal and excitement. Research has shown that music and sounds with a slow rhythmic beat induces the slow brainwave patterns, called Alpha and Theta, that are associated with calmness. Alpha brainwaves cycle at a frequency of 7–13 Hertz. This is the brainwave pattern of activity we have prior to sleeping. On the other hand Theta brainwave activity, 4–6 Hertz, is seen in deep relaxation and meditative states, and in daydreaming. Researchers have shown that music inducing Alpha and Theta brainwave activity can lead to a decrease in blood pressure and heart rate, reduced muscle tension, decrease in cortisol and an improved immune function.

Selecting the type of music and sound to achieve a therapeutic effect or a state of calmness is very much an individual choice. What works for one person may not work for another. The important point is that you enjoy the type of music. Often familiar music seems to be the most effective. Common types of effective music for relaxation are slow, repetitive drum beats, flute, Celtic, Native American Indian, Raga (Indian classical), chanting, Baroque, New Age, classical pieces, slow jazz, slow harp and the sounds of nature (forest, waves, waterfalls, bird song). Some specific examples are:

▶ *Saku*, Susumu Yokota
▶ *Nocturne*, Chopin
▶ Mozart's *Eine kleine Nachtmusik, Divertimento No. 2 in D Major, Sonata for two pianos in D major*, second movement
▶ *Canon in D*, Pachelbel

- *The Rose*, Aoi Teshima
- *By This River*, Brian Eno
- *Pie Jesu*, John Rutter
- *Albatross*, Fleetwood Mac
- *Bridge over Troubled Water*, Simon and Garfunkel
- *Piano concerto No. 1*, Tchaikovsky
- *Romance*, Dvorak
- *Brahms' Lullaby*.

Music can enhance the experience of relaxation of other relaxing activities. So, listening to your favourite, soothing music while savouring the warmth of an aromatherapy bath might be the best way for you to relax.

Aromatherapy

This is restorative treatment or phytotherapy by the use of essential oils and fragrances. Aromatherapy is a general term used to describe any application of essential oils for wellbeing.

An essential oil is a highly volatile fat formed in specialized cells in plants. The essential oil can be found in the roots, leaves, flowers, bark or in the skin of fruits. The oil is extracted by a chemical distillation process, whereby steam is passed over the plant material in a still and the essential oil is extracted from the steam which has been condensed into water.

Oils are most commonly used in burners, soaked into tissue or in massage. The claimed benefits of aromatherapy include improved mood, sleep, circulation, digestion and diuresis. In addition, there appear to be significant antibiotic, anti-fungal, anti-inflammatory and analgesic effects. There is evidence to suggest that these effects appear to operate at pharmacological, as well as psychobiological levels.

Pharmacological effects are thought to be due to the molecular properties of the specific aromatherapy ingredient, e.g. linalool, which is the main component of lavender oil, can readily cross the blood-brain barrier, acting to inhibit the action of certain neurotransmitters at synapses. It can thus act as a narcotic. The anaesthetizing effects of lavender oil are due to linalool being able to block ion channels locally, in the neuron cell membrane. Anti-inflammatory effects appear to be due to blocking effects, by linalool, of functional proteins in the cell membrane of mast cells (cells of the immune system) which are responsible for inflammation.

Psychological effects appear to depend on how the odour of the oil is perceived according to two variables – the concentration of the odour (and the mode of usage) and by association. Evidence shows that a relatively high concentration of most odours can be considered unpleasant and can impair performance, while relatively low concentrations of odours can be considered pleasant and can enhance performance. Further, association or a learned experience of an odour with some event or object can affect response. Particular odours may have a strong negative or positive association and may be expected to influence outcome measures in research studies, operating through the individual's emotional systems. Such variables should always be controlled in studies of odorant effects on behaviour.

There is no doubt that essential oils exert significant psychobiological and pharmacological effects. There is much to be gained from using these natural compounds in phytotherapy. It is very important to understand the detail about essential oil composition to ensure proper and correct application. Such detailed knowledge is currently not available, so although we advocate the use of essential oils, the best course of action would seem to be to proceed with the use of essential oils but do so with caution. Use only high quality sources and do not exceed stated quantities.

Orthomolecular vitamin redox regimes

Orthomolecular medicine is the practice of using natural dietary substances for good health and for the treatment of disease, with emphasis on individual variability.

The current controversy about Vitamin C and its claimed health benefits is worth considering. It is a fact, and there is a long history to the finding, that Vitamin C is a potent anti-cancer substance, acting as an antioxidant as well as having other health benefits, namely acting as an anti-inflammatory.

Vitamin C gets into tumour cells and causes a build-up of hydrogen peroxide (nature's equivalent to bleach) which kills unhealthy cells by oxidizing them. This discovery has been known since the 1960s when it was found by the double Nobel Prize winner, Linus Pauling, that Vitamin C selectively kills cancer cells without harming normal ones. Only now are trials beginning, using human patients, to test for safety and tolerance of treatment for cancer using Vitamin C.

Cancer is the abnormal growth of abnormal cells. Tumours can occur because the abnormal cells divide more rapidly and refuse to die. Antioxidants can prevent cancer by inhibiting cell division, so the tumour does not grow and cells die. Cell division and cell death are controlled, in part, by the balance of antioxidants (reducing agents) and oxidants (oxidizing agents) – hence the term redox.

While research in redox regimes focuses primarily on diet and cancer, the findings are also of enormous benefit for stress management because of effects on the stress response. Deficiencies of any one of the following causes DNA damage in the cell: folic acid, Vitamin B6, Vitamin B12, Vitamin B3, Vitamin C, Vitamin E, iron and zinc. In principle, deficiencies in the diet greatly increase the chances of poor coping with stress. This is especially so in the case of antioxidant vitamins and minerals. For body cells to remain healthy, good nutrition is essential. The researchers point out that 'cells do not live by Vitamin C alone'. Other nutritional factors are needed to prevent ill health, including other vitamins, minerals, amino acids, fatty acids, phytonutrients and oxygen.

Currently there is one self-help guide available, written by Drs Steven Hickey and Hilary Roberts offering practical information to control many cancers by dietary means. In so doing, this guide is also an excellent guide and an invaluable tool in stress management planning. So called 'redox-active' nutrients offer the promise not only of a safe anti-cancer therapy, which may be more effective than current chemotherapy, but also a practical and objective way of maintaining a balanced nutritional body state, hence increasing resilience for dealing with stressors.

The following regime for good nutrition is published with the kind permission of Hickey and Roberts (2007, page 241):

'Good nutrition is an accepted part of cancer prevention. In particular, a low carbohydrate diet with a high intake of vegetables could be beneficial. Antioxidant supplementation may reduce the risk of developing cancer:

- *Vitamin C (as L-ascorbic acid) – dynamic flow level, half a gram or more, 5–6 times a day*
- *R-alpha-lipoic acid – 50–100 mg, twice daily*
- *Vitamin D3 – 100IU per day*
- *selenium – 200 μg per day*
- *absorbable magnesium – 200–400 mg per day as magnesium citrate or magnesium chelate*
- *Vitamin E – 400IU per day, preferably mixed natural tocopherols and tocotrienols*
- *good general nutritional supplement support (e.g. multivitamins and minerals)*
- *cut down on sugars (e.g. no sugar in tea or coffee), cakes and biscuits*
- *low carbohydrate diet*
- *choose colourful, low carbohydrate vegetables (containing antioxidants).'*

Appendix III: *Stresswise* products

Products available from *Stresswise* include:

- ▶ *Biodots*
- ▶ *Self-adhesive red hearts*
- ▶ Stresswise *heart clip*
- ▶ Stresswise *relaxation tape (including ten Biodots)*

Products referred to in this book are available online from:

www.stresswise.com or by writing to:

Stresswise
PO Box 96
Holyhead
LL65 9BA

E-mail: stresswise@talk21.com

For full product list and descriptions, current prices and contact details visit the website www.stresswise.com.

Taking it further

Further reading

Bloom, W., *The Endorphin Effect: A Breakthrough Strategy for Holistic Health and Spiritual Wellbeing* (Piatkus, 2000).

Cooper, J. and Lewis, J., *Who can I talk to? The user's guide to therapy and counselling* (Hodder and Stoughton, 1995).

Ernst, E. et al, *The Oxford Handbook of Complementary Medicine* (Oxford University Press, 2008).

Friedman, M. and Rosenman, R., *Type A Behaviour and your Heart* (Wildwood House Ltd/Fawcett, 1974).

Friedman, M. and Ulmer, D., *Treating Type A Behaviour and your Heart* (Alfred A. Knopf, 1984).

Friedman, M., *Type A Behaviour: its diagnosis and treatment* (Plenum Press, 1996).

Hickey, S. and Roberts, H., *The cancer breakthrough: a nutritional approach for doctors and patients* (Lulu Press, 2007; available from www.lulu.com).

Holford, P., *The Optimum Nutrition Bible* (Piatkus, 1997).

Kendrick, M., *The great cholesterol con* (John Blake, 2007).

Kraus, B. and Reilly-Pardo, M., *Calories and Carbohydrates* (Signet Books, 2001).

Leader, D. and Corfield, D., *Why do people get ill?* (Hamish Hamilton, 2007).

Pasternak, C.A., *The Molecules Within us: Our Body in Health and Disease* (Plenum, 1998).

Payne, R., *Relaxation Techniques* (Churchill Livingstone, 1995).

Pert, C.B., *Molecules of Emotion: Why you feel the way you feel* (Simon and Schuster, 1997).

Piper, B., *Diet and Nutrition* (Chapman and Hall, 1996).

Sapolsky, R., *Why Zebras don't get Ulcers: a guide to stress-related diseases and coping* (W.H. Freeman and Company, 1994).

Singh, S. and Ernst, E., *Trick or Treatment? Alternative Medicine on Trial* (Bantam, 2008).

Taylor, M.T. and McGee, S., *The New Couple. Why the old rules don't work and what does* (Harper, 2000).

Widmaier, E.P., *Why Geese Don't Get Obese and We Do* (W.H. Freeman, 1998).

Other books in the *Teach Yourself* series that complement *Manage Your Stress for a Happier Life*:

Change Your Mood with Aromatherapy
Lose Weight, Gain Energy, Get Healthy
Help Yourself to Live Longer
Get Started in Massage
Beat Stress with Meditation
Relaxation Techniques
Relax and Unwind with Yoga

Websites

www.stresswise.com – Stress management products: Biodots, relaxation tape, massagers and reminder devices.

www.waystounwind.com – A directory of products, activities and services designed to help you unwind, with information on stress and its management.

www.isma.org.uk – International Stress Management Association (UK) site provides a list of stress management consultants, useful links and resource material.

www.eatwell.gov.uk – Food Standard Agency website.

www.bbc.co.uk/health/mental/stress.shtml – First-class site from the BBC, packed with information on health, covering the lifestyle issues dealt with in this book.

www.bbc.co.uk/headroom – Site for the campaign to encourage you to look after your mental wellbeing. Wellbeing guides, videos and assessments.

www.mhf.org.uk – Mental Health Foundation site provides information on mental health, including sleep, and links to resource material. Good booklet: Cool Down – anger and how to deal with it. Podcasts and downloads.

www.mind.org.uk – Mental health charity site with access to useful factsheets.

www.samaritans.org.uk – Helpful guidance and advice for those with severe anxiety and depression and need someone to talk with.

www.ash.org.uk – Action on smoking and health.
www.ash.org – US site for action on smoking and health.
www.relate.org.uk – Site dealing with relationship counselling.
www.aa.org – US site for alcoholics anonymous.

www.nrhp.co.uk – Site of the National Register of Hypnotherapists and Psychotherapists.

www.weightlossresources.co.uk – Online calorie and nutrition database.

www.caloriecounter.co.uk – Useful resource site for bodyweight control.

www.bdaweightwise.com – British Dietetic Association website where you can calculate your ideal body weight and learn how to manage your weight.

www.bhf.org.uk – British Heart Foundation site. See 'Keeping a healthy heart'.

www.stocksurgery.co.uk – Family GP practice website, with a lot of helpful information and guidance on health issues and lifestyle. Some useful assessments.

www.nlpacademy.co.uk – Neuro liguistic programming website.

www.britishhypnotherapists.org.uk – British hypnotherapists' site.

Index